CAN WE TALK?

A Multiskills Approach
To Communication

CAN WE TALK?

A Multiskills Approach
To Communication

DONALD R.H. BYRD
JOHN KLOSEK

PRENTICE HALL REGENTS Englewood Cliffs, New Jersey 07632

Library of Congress Cataloging-in-Publication Data

Byrd, Donald R. H.
    Can we talk? : a multiskills approach to communication / Donald
R.H. Byrd, John Klosek.
        p.   cm.
    ISBN 0-13-114166-X (pbk.) :
    1. English language--Textbooks for foreign speakers.
2. Communication.   I. Klosek, John, 1950-   . II. Title.
PE1128.B84 1991
428.2'4--dc20   90-14195
                                                     CIP

Editorial/production supervision
and interior design: **Shirley Hinkamp**
Cover design: **Richard Puder**
Pre-press buyer: **Ray Keating**
Manufacturing buyer: **Lori Bulwin**
Photo Research: **Page Poore**
Illustrations: **Len Shalansky**

© 1991 by Prentice-Hall, Inc.
A Division of Simon & Schuster
Englewood Cliffs, New Jersey 07632

Printed in the United States of America
10 9 8 7 6 5 4 3 2 1

ISBN 0-13-114166-X

Prentice-Hall International (UK) Limited, *London*
Prentice-Hall of Australia Pty. Limited, *Sydney*
Prentice-Hall Canada Inc., *Toronto*
Prentice-Hall Hispanoamericana, S.A., *Mexico*
Prentice-Hall of India Private Limited, *New Delhi*
Prentice-Hall of Japan, Inc., *Tokyo*
Simon & Schuster Asia Pte. Ltd., *Singapore*
Editora Prentice-Hall do Brasil, Ltda., *Rio de Janeiro*

CONTENTS

Unit/Title	Topic	Functions/(Structures)	
1. The Case of the Sick Snake	Mystery of a circus crime	Identifying professions, nationalities; talking about languages (*be* + professions, *be* + location; present continuous)	1
2. How's the Weather?	Weather and personality	Talking about likes and dislikes, activities (*like to, don't like to; be/feel* + adjective)	11
3. Free Time	Hobbies	Comparing; giving reasons (*I think* + *NP* + *be* + *better*; present continuous; possessive nouns)	21
4. Fountain of Youth	Personal appearance	Describing before and after appearance; giving reasons; (*look, feel* + comparative; present tense— third person singular; past tense)	29
5. Where's Tweetie?	Mystery about pets	Comparing before and after conditions; identifying; expressing probability; (*be*+location, *maybe*; past tense positive and negative)	39
6. Games People Play	Sports	Stating the rules of a game (*wh-* questions); comparing and giving opinions (*better, safer*)	45

TO THE STUDENT

In your own language you are able to express your ideas and opinions. You can understand others. You can use your language as a tool. *Can We Talk?* lets you do the same things in English. It invites you to communicate in English.

Students of English usually understand much more than they can say. *Can We Talk?* takes advantage of this ability. Each unit begins with pictures that give the topic and vocabulary you will need later. Communication activities allow you to interact with your classmates. First, you discuss what is in the unit, and then you express your own ideas and opinions with each other.

You don't have to worry about making mistakes. Mistakes are normal in language learning. You can learn from them. Confidence in expressing your ideas in English is really more important than always being correct. Confidence builds fluency. *Can We Talk?* will help you become more fluent in English.

Communication always requires two or more people. You will not learn to communicate in English by yourself. In most classes, the teacher, other students, and you take turns speaking. *Can We Talk?* gives you opportunities to work together in pairs and small groups. We know that the more you practice together, the more you will learn.

Can We Talk? covers topics that are interesting to everyone:

small talk (the weather, free time, leisure activities, sensitivity to others' feelings)
health (youth and appearance, minor and major health problems)
clued mysteries (missing canary, stolen jewelry, burglary, hijacking, murder, and
    blackmail)
dilemmas (pollution, bribery, personal values, drunk driving, money and lifestyle,
    gambling)

Can We Talk? practices many language functions, the reasons why we communicate. Typical functions include expressing feelings; talking about possibility and probability; making predictions; giving advice; describing appearance, stating preferences; making moral judgments; agreeing and disagreeing; comparing situations and people; giving reasons; discussing priorities; reporting conversations, facts, statistics, and conditions; and relating a series of events.

Grammar and vocabulary are also important in communication. Most students don't really like grammar and vocabulary, however, because they are often boring. In *Can We Talk?* grammar and vocabulary are tools. They are means to an end. They lead the way to communication. In other words, they prepare you to express your own opinions and feelings about interesting, everyday topics.

Most people have their own ideas on the topics in this book. Often these ideas conflict. In most cases, there are no right or wrong answers. It is important to listen to the views of others and to respect them.

TO THE TEACHER

Can We Talk?: A Multiskills Approach to Communication is for students of English who have some knowledge of the basic structures, functions, and vocabulary. *Can We Talk?*, however, provides these students with a number of situations to express their ideas, opinions, and emotions on a variety of topics. Furthermore, students are expected to use their associative abilities to figure out dilemmas, mysteries, and arrange priorities. At all times, the emphasis is on the expression of one's own thoughts in English rather than on isolated points of grammar or vocabulary.

Can We Talk? enables students to interact meaningfully during the early stages of acquiring English by exploiting the commonality of human experience. Therefore, the situations included in this book draw on various topics and themes that are contemporary, engaging, and international in perspective.

Graphics, realia, charts, tables, illustrations, and photographs are carefully integrated into learning activities so that a maximum of content (through art) is conveyd with a minimum of language. Furthermore, this graphic support stimulates individualized learning for later comparison with other members of the class. In this way, *Can We Talk?* assures a dynamic, interactive classroom.

At the beginning level, language comprehension is probably more important than language production, but production is the ultimate goal. Students, in general, are able to understand far more than they can say. In order to take advantage of this reception-production dichotomy, the tasks in *Can We Talk?* follow a sequence:

1. Students are exposed to new vocabulary or content through tasks that require mere recognition or manipulation of the material.
2. After the students are familiar with the material, they are guided to produce it in speech.
3. Later, reading and writing activities reinforce this sequence.

The activities in *Can We Talk?* are teacher set, but not teacher centered. The students must be allowed to explore their own feelings and reactions nonjudgmentally and sympathetically. The teacher should see himself or herself as manager-expeditor-facilitator and should be prepared to relinquish control so that students will express themselves freely. The teacher is an understanding source of information and guidance but does not dominate.

There are 19 units in this book. The activities in these units are designed to engage the students personally in making value decisions, solving mysteries from clues, finding logical solutions to dilemmas, and expressing the various nuances of language in a social context. Topics include various mysteries about crimes, weather and personality, hobbies and free time, personal appearance, sports, personal belongings and values, health, winning a lot of money, gambling, bribery, environment, life-threatening emergencies, telling the truth, and driving and drinking.

Each unit is divided into the following sections:

Let's Look at It

Each unit begins with a group of three motivating questions to stimulate the students' interest in the topic. At this point, the emphasis should be on the students' shared experiences and prior knowledge, and not on grammatical correctness. Precision in expression and vocabulary will be treated in later exercises.

The teacher should briefly lead the entire class in discussing the various reactions to these questions. The pace should be lively and spontaneous.

Following the prediscussion questions is the visual layout that encapsulates the essence of the unit through the use of illustrations, drawings, photos, or realia. Students need to spend a few minutes looking over these art presentations so that they understand what is happening. Often the art is accompanied by a brief narrative or dialogue to focus further the central issue of the unit. These dialogues or narratives can be read as a teacher-guided activity. Students can take roles for dialogues and can read silently other passages.

Vocabulary

In order to talk about the topics represented in each unit, students will need "access" vocabulary, those essential words that are specific to the situational context. Receptive tasks emphasize word meanings, associations, and general comprehension of the content, and they build familiarity in a cumulative way. The access words in these exercises are always treated as they relate specifically to the unit.

Teachers should view these exercises as a means to an end: verbal interaction about the topic. Students can do these exercises in a number of ways: individually, in pairs, or in groups. If the exercises are done individually, be sure to allow the students to compare and discuss their answers with a partner or in groups.

Let's Talk about It

Authentic communication is the central focus of this section. Levels of increasingly productive tasks allow the students to express their personal views, proceeding from guided to less guided activities. Students gain confidence in their ability to communicate in English by going through this sequence of activities. They also learn specific language functions like agreeing, disagreeing, expressing opinions, making choices, reporting, giving advice, and others found in the index (page 174). Intrinsic to these functions are the correct grammatical forms, naturally carried and integrated into a communicative framework. Activities culminate in the synthetic exercise requiring group consensus or a solution to a dilemma or mystery. Many units have an Opinion Survey, where students agree or disagree with provocative statements designed to elicit value judgments, resulting in lively discussions of conflicting views.

Teachers should have students work in small groups or in pairs since these topics, usually controversial, stimulate an exchange of different or similar opinions. There is no correct answer to most of these discussions (except perhaps the mysteries) so the teacher is not burdened to play an omniscient role. Similarly, teachers should be careful not to impose their own values on the students. With sensitive teacher handling, students will learn to appreciate and understand the views of others even if those views conflict with their own. Most class time should be spent on this section.

Let's Write about It

Writing and composing exercises recycle the salient points from the previous discussion. Here, too, there is a sequence: the first exercises, controlled in nature, usually reinforce in writing some grammatical or functional item from the discussion. The last activity is usually a composing task, more open ended in nature. These writing and composing exercises are best assigned as homework.

Let's Read about It

An "authentic" reading selection in the form of a newspaper article, editorial, or letter relates to the theme of the unit. Following the reading is a series of reception and production exercises testing comprehension and vocabulary. These readings provide more information about some aspect of the topic and expand the students' awareness. They provide excellent "fillers" for those leftover ten or fifteen minutes in class after a discussion. Alternatively, the teacher may assign these readings for homework.

A Word about Group Work

"Never do yourself what a student can do" is the advice of Mary Finocchiaro to English language teachers. Remember those words when using the material in *Can We Talk?* since the materials are aimed at maximum student participation. They work best under the judicious use of the teacher, who is willing to delegate control to students. Teachers have to trust students. They must also have confidence in the students' abilities to associate ideas, to experiment with English expression, and to monitor themselves for correctness, for fluency rests on these abilities. However, there may be times when the teacher will have to intercede if one or two students tend to dominate. Here are some general suggestions for getting students to participate without teacher control.

Individuals: Set students to work on a task silently. Keep such activities brief. Proceed to pair or group work as soon as possible since the ultimate goal is to have students compare their work and interact orally.

Pairs: Pair work guarantees the greatest amount of student participation and allows for a two-way exchange of ideas. A good way to form random pairs is to have students count off going around the room. Students with the closest odd numbers (1 and 3, 5 and 7, and so on) form pairs and, similarly, students with the closest even numbers (2 and 4, 6 and 8, and so on) form pairs. If, however, the teacher wants to mix abilities or languages, he or she can ask specific individuals to work together. To be sure that everyone is "on task," the teacher must monitor the pairs by circulating quietly around the room. Time allocations for pair work range from five minutes (for some vocabulary tasks) to twenty minutes (for some extended discussion tasks).

Groups: Although there is relatively less individual participation in groups, there is considerably more exchange of ideas. Students in groups have the opportunity to communicate with more and different kinds of people, simulating the real world. Group skills include negotiating and persuasion and depend on the appropriate sociolinguistic behaviors like turn taking, interrupting, and asking for clarification. Group activities are appropriate for various consensus tasks, such as the Opinion Surveys and other task types in *Can We Talk?* and can go on for longer periods of time.

UNIT 1

THE CASE OF
THE SICK SNAKE

Let's Look at It

Why is a circus exciting?
What kinds of people work in a circus?
What kinds of animals are there in a circus?

JULIETTA
EUROPE'S MOST
FAMOUS CLOWN

THE GREAT
CHANGS

TRAPEZE
ARTISTS
FROM ASIA

AZIZ
AND
AMIRA

EXTRAORDINARY
ACROBATS FROM
AFRICA

CIRCUS

3

VOCABULARY

A.   Match the following:

_____	1. international	a.	first language
_____	2. boa constrictor	b.	kind of snake
_____	3. bilingual	c.	a person who does athletic performances high in the air
_____	4. mother tongue	d.	not afraid, courageous
_____	5. magician	e.	a person who does magic
_____	6. trapeze artist	f.	using two languages
_____	7. brave	g.	from all over the world
_____	8. acrobat	h.	a person who does athletic performances by running, jumping, and flipping his or her body

B.   Complete these sentences.

1.   A person who trains animals is an _____ _____.

2.   A person who does athletic performances high in the air is a _____

_____.

3.   A magician is a person who performs _____ tricks.

4.   People who do athletic performances by running and flipping their bodies are called

_____.

5.   A _____ is a person in a circus who makes people laugh.

6.   A person from Asia is called an _____.

7.   A person from Europe is called a _____.

8.   A person from North America is a _____ _____.

Let's Talk about It

I speak Italian
at home.

Our native language
is Cantonese.

I speak both
French and English,
the languages of
my country.

We're bilingual
in French and Arabic.

My first language
is English but I'm
not European or
North American.

Portuguese is
my mother tongue,
but I'm not
from Europe.

Ssss

A. Write the names of the circus performers under their pictures. Look back at the previous page if necessary. Compare your answers.

B.   Where are the performers from? Answer the following questions.

EXAMPLE: *Who is from Asia? The Changs are from Asia.*

1.   Who is from Asia?
2.   Who is from Europe?
3.   Who is from North America?
4.   Who is from Africa?
5.   Who is from South America?
6.   Where is the ringmaster from?

C.   Give the origin of each performer.

EXAMPLE: *The Changs are Asian.*

D.   Which country do you think the performers are from?

EXAMPLE: *I think the Changs are from China because they speak Cantonese.*

1.   What about Julietta, the clown?
2.   What about Michel, the animal trainer?
3.   What about Madame Zara, the magician?
4.   What about Theodore, the ringmaster?
5.   What about Aziz and Amira?
6.   What about Homer, the boa constrictor?

E.   Madame Zara and Homer are next to perform. Homer is eating his food as usual—just before the performance. Then Madame Zara notices that Homer is getting sick and sleepy. She finds poison in Homer's food. She knows no one likes Homer. She quickly looks around her. This is what she sees:

• One of the Africans is exercising.
• The trapeze artists are high in the air.
• The North American performer is speaking French with a female performer.
• A female performer is putting on more make-up.
• The monolingual English speaker is helping Madame Zara.

Answer these questions:

1.   Who is performing now?
2.   Who is *not* performing now?
3.   Who is the next person or persons to perform?
4.   What are Aziz and Amira doing?
5.   Who is speaking French together?
6.   What is the ringmaster doing?
7.   Who did it? Who put the poison in Homer's food?
8.   How do you think this person did it?

Let's Write about It

A. Write sentences about the nationalities and languages of five performers.

EXAMPLE: *The Changs are from China and speak Cantonese.*

1. _____

2. _____

3. _____

4. _____

5. _____

B. Write about what the performers are doing when Madame Zara looks around.

EXAMPLE: *The Changs are performing high in the air.*

1. _____

2. _____

3. _____

4. _____

5. _____

C. Write in the missing parts of Madame Zara's letter.

It was awful. (1) _____ almost died. Someone (2) _____

poison in his food just (3) _____ our performance. And I know who did it. I was

(4) _____ to Theodore, but I saw the other performers. (5) _____

and (6) _____ were (7) _____ French together. (8) _____

was exercising. The (9) _____ family were performing (10) _____

in the air. The only person near Homer was (11) _____. That's who did it, and it's
not funny.

Let's Read about It

Snake Facts

Are you afraid of snakes, too? Most people are. They are such cold, ugly animals.

Why don't people like snakes? Maybe it's the small green eyes and the forked tongue. Or maybe it's the way they move—so quietly and mysteriously. They don't make much noise. Maybe it's their history. You do remember, don't you, that it was a snake that tempted Eve in the garden of Eden? The world is no longer the same.

Some snakes are very poisonous. The poison of an Indian cobra, an American coral snake, or a Texas rattler can kill you in a few seconds—if you do not get help. Other snakes like South American boa constrictors and Asian pythons do not have poison, but they kill in another way: They squeeze you to death by wrapping around you until you stop breathing.

Not all snakes are dangerous. There are 2,700 kinds of snakes in the world, and only 20 percent of these are really dangerous. What about the size of snakes? They range in length from 4 inches (10 centimeters) to 30 feet (90 meters), and, surprisingly, some of the most poisonous ones are small.

Most snakes are helpful. They eat insects and mice, and some people eat snakes. In Asia and Texas, for example, snake meat is a rare treat to some people. In the elegant shops of Paris, Tokyo, Rio, New York, or Milan, you can buy belts, shoes, and handbags made from snake skin.

If you are really afraid of snakes, go to Ireland or New Zealand. They are the only countries in the world that have no snakes at all.

EXERCISES

A. Circle the word that is different.

1. Rio	Milan	Asia
2. belts	shoes	mice
3. Ireland	Texas	New Zealand
4. poisonous	dangerous	helpful
5. forked tongue	poisonous	green eyes
6. quietly	mysteriously	ugly

B. *True or false?*

_____ 1. The writer is afraid of snakes.

_____ 2. New Zealand has only nonpoisonous snakes.

_____ 3. Most snakes are *not* poisonous.

_____ 4. Of all the kinds of snakes, only about 540 are poisonous.

_____ 5. Snakes only kill with poison.

_____ 6. A boa constrictor is a poisonous snake.

C. Answer these questions.
1. How are snakes helpful?
2. How many kinds of snakes are there in the world?
3. Which countries have *no* snakes? Why?
4. Why do most people dislike snakes?
5. How do snakes kill?

UNIT 2

HOW'S THE WEATHER?

Let's Look at It

How do you feel on a sunny day?
When it's raining, how do you feel?
When it's hot and humid, how do you feel?

A In the Sahara Desert

B In the jungle

C In Chicago

D In Scandinavia

E At the South Pole

VOCABULARY

A. Match the expressions with a picture. Each picture has more than one expression.

_____ 1. It's raining.

_____ 2. It's sunny.

_____ 3. It's windy.

_____ 4. It's cold.

_____ 5. It's hot.

_____ 6. It's humid.

_____ 7. It's snowing.

_____ 8. It's cloudy.

_____ 9. It's cool.

B. Circle the correct answer.

1. It's easy to fly a kite when the wind is [a) windy, b) blowing, c) sunny].
2. The beach is nice when the sun is [a) cold, b) raining, c) shining].
3. [a) How's, b) What's, c) Why's] the weather like in Chicago?
4. It's [a) hot and humid, b) cold and rainy, c) sunny and windy] in the jungle.
5. I like to [a) go camping, b) fly a kite, c) ski] when it's snowing.
6. I don't like to cook when the weather is [a) cold, b) hot, c) cool].
7. I like to sleep late when it's [a) raining, b) hot, c) humid].
8. Some families go on picnics on [a) Monday, b) Friday, c) Sunday].
9. [a) Spring, b) Winter, c) Fall] is a good time to fly a kite.

Let's Talk about It

A.   Say what you *like* or *don't like* to do from the following list. Use a weather expression when possible. Talk about other things you *like* or *don't like* to do.

EXAMPLES: *I like to cook when it's cool.*
I don't like to cook when it's hot.
I like to play cards anytime.
I don't like to clean house anytime.

1. swim
2. ski
3. read
4. jog
5. fly a kite
6. sleep late
7. play tennis/cards/basketball/football
8. watch television/a parade/a football game
9. go camping/on a picnic/to the beach/shopping
10. clean house/my room
11. work in the garden/on my homework
12. get up early

B. SEASONS: Play a game. One person says a word associated with a season (spring, summer, fall, winter) and another person names the season. Continue around the room until someone misses. When a person doesn't answer or answers incorrectly, that person drops out. The last person to ask is the winner.

EXAMPLE: *first person: flower*   *second person: spring*
　　　　　　　second person: snow   *third person: winter*
　　　　　　　third person: leaves   *fourth person: ?*

C. INTERVIEW: Choose *six* of the following questions. With a partner, practice asking and answering them. Report your partner's answers.

QUESTIONNAIRE

1. What do you like to do when it's hot/cold/sunny/windy/raining/snowing?

2. What don't you like to do when it's hot/cold/sunny/windy/raining/snowing?

3. What kind of weather do you like best?

4. What kind of weather do you dislike most?

5. What is your favorite season?

6. What do you like to do during your favorite kind of weather?

7. What do you like to do during your favorite season?

8. What is the weather like in your country?

9. Which seasons do you have in your country?

10. In your country, which months are in each season?

Let's Write about It

A. Likes and Dislikes
1. Write one thing you like to do and one thing you don't like to do when it's raining.

    a. _____

    b. _____

2. Write one thing you like to do and one thing you don't like to do on a sunny day.

    a. _____

    b. _____

3. Choose a season. Write one thing you like to do and one thing you don't like to do during that season.

    a. _____

    b. _____

4. How do you feel when _____?

EXAMPLE: *it's sunny? I feel happy when it's sunny.*

a. the sun is shining?_____

b. it's raining?_____

c. it's cold?_____

d. it's snowing?_____

B.   Write an answer to the following letter. Discuss the weather in your country or city. Use the letter as an example.

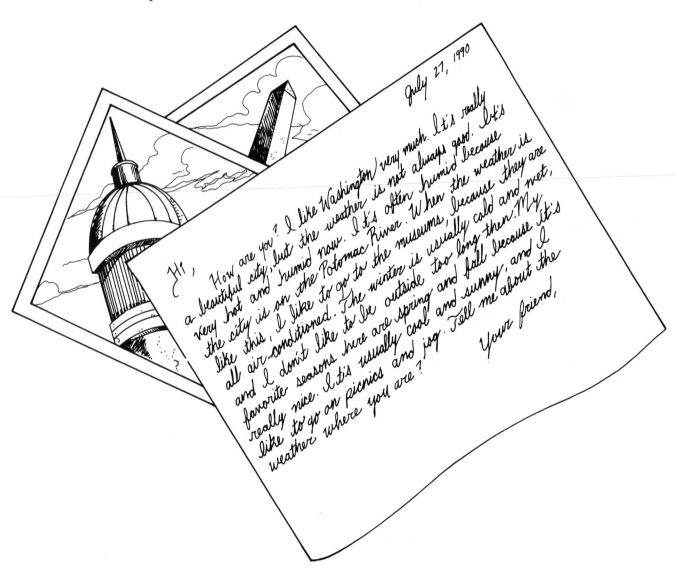

July 27, 1990

Hi,

How are you? I like Washington very much. It's really a beautiful city, but the weather is not always good. It's very hot and humid now. It's often humid because the city is on the Potomac River. When the weather is like this, I like to go to the museums, because they are all air-conditioned. The winter is usually cold and wet, and I don't like to be outside too long then. My favorite seasons here are spring and fall because it's really nice. It's usually cool and sunny, and I like to go on picnics and jog. Tell me about the weather where you are?

Your friend,

_____

_____

_____

_____

_____

_____

_____

Let's Read about It

How's the Weather?

Will Rogers, an American humorist, said, "Everyone talks about the weather, but no one does anything about it." He was right. People talk about the weather all the

5   time. A person who wants to start a conversation usually says something like: "Nice day, isn't it?" or "Whew, it's hot today" or "Brr, it's cold!" Almost always the other person, friend or stranger, expresses agreement

10   with a response like: "It sure is."

The weather affects our personality. We are usually in good spirits on sunny days. On rainy, dark days, we sometimes get depressed or feel "blue." In "Stormy Weather,"

15   a famous blues song, W. C. Handy talks about his sadness because "it just keeps raining all the time."

Psychologists know that sunlight is im-portant for good health. In dark areas near the Arctic Circle, some people get de-   20 pressed during the long, dark winters. "Light therapy," three or four hours of bright light each day, usually brings them back to normal.

The weather sets a mood, too, espe-   25 cially for a scary story. Do scary stories happen in sunny weather? Rain and wind make any story a little scarier. Any story that begins with "It was a dark and rainy night . . ." brings a chill down our backs.   30

Sun and warmth make us feel happy and optimistic. It's a little difficult to be optimistic on a cloudy day, but on a nice, sunny day, there are very few pessimists around. That sounds like something Will Rogers said,   35 doesn't it?

EXERCISES

A. Find the word that is different.
1. a) blue b) depressed c) sunny
2. a) dark b) optimistic c) sunny
3. a) Whew b) Brr c) Sure
4. a) warm b) chill c) scary
5. a) cloudy b) dark c) sunny
6. a) usually b) sometimes c) always

B. Circle the correct answer.
1. People often [a) finish, b) continue, c) start] a conversation by talking about the weather.
2. Most people are [a) optimistic, b) pessimistic, c) blue] on a sunny day.
3. "It sure is" is a way of [a) talking about the weather, b) agreeing, c) expressing optimism].
4. In the song, W. C. Handy feels sad because of the [a) sunny, b) rainy, c) cloudy] weather.
5. Will Rogers was [a) a psychologist, b) a pessimist, c) a humorist].
6. [a) Sunlight, b) Winter, c) Therapy] is important for our health.

C. Complete the following sentences.

1. We are in good spirits on _____ days.

2. It's difficult _____ on a cloudy day.

3. _____, there aren't many pessimists around.

4. "Everyone _____, but no one does anything about it."

5. A good way to start a conversation is to say, "_____."

6. "It was a dark and rainy night" is a good beginning for _____.

7. People who live near the Arctic Circle become depressed during _____.

8. _____ usually brings the person back to normal.

UNIT 3

FREE TIME

Let's Look at It

Do you have any hobbies?
What do you like to do in your free time?
What free-time activity would you recommend to a friend?

VOCABULARY

A. Who is doing these things?

_____	1. knitting a sweater	a.	an older woman
_____	2. playing golf	b.	a family
_____	3. hiking in the woods	c.	a football player
_____	4. reading a book	d.	two men
_____	5. hunting ducks	e.	two women
_____	6. working with wood	f.	an older man
_____	7. painting a landscape	g.	a man and a woman
_____	8. collecting antiques	h.	a child

B.   Work with a partner. One person will read an *answer* and the other will ask a *question*. Take turns.

1.   "It's so relaxing. I can make such nice sweaters and scarves with my hands."

EXAMPLE: Answer: *"It's so relaxing. I can make such nice sweaters and scarves with my hands."*
Question: *Why do you like to knit?*

2.   "I feel so proud when I make something with my hands, and I like the touch and smell of wood."
3.   "It's a challenge—just to see if I can capture the beauty on paper."
4.   "It gives us a chance to bring home extra food."
5.   "It's a way to make some extra money. We buy an old piece, work on it, and then sell it at a profit."
6.   "I learn a lot and I get many new ideas."
7.   "We love the outdoors. We share the beauties of nature as a family."
8.   "It's a lot of fun. We're not professionals, but we're kind of serious about the game."

Let's Talk about It

A.   What is each person doing in the picture? Why does each one like it?

EXAMPLE: *The football player is knitting. He likes it because it is relaxing.*

B.   Which leisure activities
• are good for young people? for old people? for people of any age?
• are done alone? with other people?
• are for men? for women? for children?
• are done outdoors? indoors? anywhere?
• are most relaxing? least relaxing?
• are most expensive? least expensive?

C.   All the people in the pictures know each other. Most are related. Can you figure out their relationships based on the words of this person? Look back at the pictures if necessary.

"I am a carpenter's daughter. My son is the grandson of a Sunday painter. My brothers-in-law like to hunt. My sister likes to collect antiques with her good friend, the wife of the man who knits for relaxation. My sister-in-law spends her free time with her family hiking."

---

1 = the male golfer   2 = the female golfer   3 = the Sunday painter
4 = the carpenter   5 = the two hunters   6 = the male hiker
7 = the female hiker   8 = the young hiker   9 = the knitter
10 = the single antique collector   11 = the married antique collector
12 = the reader

Fill in the numbers for each person and then explain their relationship.

a _____ The speaker's mother   g _____ The speaker's sister-in-law
b _____ The speaker's father   h _____ The speaker's brother
c _____ The speaker's brothers-in-law i _____ The speaker's nephew
d _____ The speaker's sister   j _____ The speaker's son
e _____ The speaker's friend   k _____ The speaker's husband
f _____ The person speaking   l _____ The sister's friend's husband

Let's Write about It

A.   Write the questions for these answers.

1.   _____ ?

It's challenging to try to get the view on paper.

2.   _____ ?

It's relaxing.

3.   _____ ?

I can learn a lot.

4.   _____ ?

We can bring home food.

5.   _____ ?

It's a chance to make a little extra money.

6.   _____ ?

I'm proud of what I make with my hands.

7. _____ ?

   It's a game we can play together.

8. _____ ?

   We can enjoy the beauties of nature as a family.

B.   What do you like to do in your free time? Write a paragraph by answering these questions.

What do you like to do in your free time?
Why do you like to do it?
When do you like to do it?
Where do you usually do it?

_____

_____

_____

_____

_____

_____

_____

_____

_____

_____

_____

Let's Read about It

Just like a Bird

The wind comes strongly up the valley to the top of the cliff. There Fletcher Eagleton waits for just the right moment to run toward the edge and jump. No, he isn't crazy. He's enjoying his hobby—hang gliding, a sport where a person holds onto a large kite and guides it down to the ground. To hang glide, you need a lot of wind and a high place to jump from.

When people think of hang gliding, they often picture a young man in the best of health. Fletcher Eagleton doesn't fit that picture. He's 75 years old, but he's in good health. His slim body is strapped securely to the glider, his head is covered with a safety helmet, and he wears running shoes. That's so he can run easily when he and his glider come down to the ground minutes later on the flat land below.

Fletcher has tried other hobbies such as motorcycle racing, for example, but hang gliding is what he likes best now. He says he likes it because he feels completely free up in the sky. "Just like a bird," he says with a smile. "For a man my age, there aren't many thrills left, but I think I've found one. Hang gliding keeps me active. Now, stand back, you young ones, and let Fletch stretch . . . his wings."

EXERCISES

A. Which line or lines in the reading give the following information?
1. The kind of equipment Fletcher has.
2. A description of Fletcher Eagleton.
3. An explanation of what hang gliding is.
4. The reasons Fletcher likes hang gliding.
5. The location and weather conditions for hang gliding.
6. Fletcher's age.

B. Answer the following questions.
1. Where do you have to go to hang glide?
2. What is unusual about Fletcher Eagleton?
3. What are the thrills of hang gliding?
4. What kind of equipment do you need?
5. What kind of people usually hang glide?
6. Do you think hang gliding is dangerous?

UNIT 4

FOUNTAIN OF YOUTH

Let's Look at It

Why do people want to look young?
What are some physical changes that happen as you get older?
What are some things that people do to look younger?

Ed   Grace

Oliver

VOCABULARY

A.   Match the following *words* with their meanings.

   _____   1.   Grace *dyes* her hair.   a.   lines on the face

   _____   2.   Bob is upset about his   b.   become thinner
                    baldness.

   _____   3.   Nina's *wrinkles* bother her.   c.   changes the color of

   _____   4.   Ed needs to *lose weight*.   d.   false teeth

   _____   5.   Chang wants new *dentures*. e.   condition of not
                                     having hair

   _____   6.   Nina wants to have a *facelift*. f.   toupee or wig

   _____   7.   Ed is *overweight*.   g.   surgery to make the
                                       face look younger

   _____   8.   Bob's *hairpiece* looks nice. h.   fat

   _____   9.   Lucy *has poor eyesight*.   i.   doesn't hear well

   _____ 10.   Oliver *is hard of hearing*. j.   doesn't see well

Nina

Bob

Lucy

Chang

B. Circle the correct answer.

1. Nina decides to [a) buy a hairpiece, b) have a facelift, c) buy a hearing aid, d) get new dentures].
2. Ed looks better after he [a) buys a hairpiece, b) loses weight, c) dyes his hair, d) has a facelift].
3. Before Grace [a) dyes her hair, b) has a facelift, c) loses weight, d) gets new glasses], she looks older.
4. Bob is upset because he [a) has so many wrinkles, b) is getting bald, c) is overweight, d) needs new dentures].
5. [a) Nina's, b) Bob's, c) Grace's, d) Ed's] condition was unhealthy.
6. Chang doesn't want to smile when he isn't wearing his [a) hairpiece, b) dentures, c) glasses, d) hearing aid].
7. Which is *not* always a sign of getting older? [a) grey hair, b) wrinkles, c) baldness, d) being overweight, e) dentures]
8. All these people think they look [a) older, b) more attractive, c) younger, d) thinner] after their changes.
9. Oliver [a) sees, b) hears, c) looks] better after buying [d) glasses, e) a hearing aid, f) dentures].
10. Lucy has difficulty [a) reading, b) hearing, c) eating, d) chewing].

Let's Talk about It

A.   Who said these things? Bob? Grace? Nina? Ed? Chang? Lucy? Oliver? Did they say these things *before* or *after* the changes? Explain your answers. Look at the pictures if necessary.

	WHO?	BEFORE	AFTER
1. "I don't like this grey hair."	_____	_____	_____
2. "I hate these wrinkles."	_____	_____	_____
3. "I'm too fat."	_____	_____	_____
4. "I think I look younger."	_____	_____	_____
5. "Why am I getting bald?"	_____	_____	_____
6. "It isn't healthy for me to be this way."	_____	_____	_____
7. "I think I'll buy a hairpiece."	_____	_____	_____
8. "I like the color."	_____	_____	_____
9. "What I need is a facelift."	_____	_____	_____
10. "Now I can eat my food properly."	_____	_____	_____
11. "My eyes are getting weak. I think I need glasses."	_____	_____	_____
12. "How do I operate this thing?"	_____	_____	_____

B.   Answer these questions.

1.   Which people had a problem with their face? eyes? hair? skin? teeth? weight? hearing? appearance?
2.   Which people had to see a(n) dentist? opthalmologist? hair stylist? cosmetic surgeon? doctor?
3.   Which changes were necessary? unnecessary?
4.   Which people look better? happier? prettier? more handsome? younger? thinner? Why do you think so?

EXAMPLE: *Bob looks younger because he's wearing a hairpiece.*

C.   As people get older, they change. In a group, discuss at least five changes that happen with age.

D. Read this list of eight problems of aging. Without talking to others, rank them in terms of seriousness (1 = very serious; 8 = not serious at all). Then, compare and discuss your answers with other students.

_____being overweight   _____baldness   _____poor hearing   _____grey hair
_____having no teeth   _____poor vision   _____poor memory   _____wrinkles

E. Circle A (agree) or D (disagree) for the following sentences. Then discuss your answers.

OPINION SURVEY

A D 1. Beauty is only skin deep.

A D 2. People worry too much about their appearance.

A D 3. It's not really necessary to be thin to be attractive.

A D 4. Older people want others to like them for their personality, not their appearance.

A D 5. Cosmetic surgery is only for serious physical problems.

A D 6. Women want to look young more than men do.

A D 7. Aging is a natural process and we cannot stop it.

A D 8. Old people who try always to look young are probably unhappy.

Let's Write about It

A. Write about the problems that each person had. Look at the pictures if necessary.

EXAMPLE: _Bob had a problem about his baldness._

1. _____

2. _____

3. _____

4. _____

5. _____

6. _____

B. Do these people look younger or better after the changes? Write about them.

EXAMPLE: *Bob looks younger because he's wearing a hairpiece.*

1. _____

2. _____

3. _____

4. _____

5. _____

6. _____

C. Rewrite the paragraph and tell what Jeremy *did* about his appearance. Change the title, too.

BEFORE   **AFTER**

Jeremy's Changes

Jeremy Bensen, almost sixty, is a fashion designer. Looking young means a lot to him. He hates getting older. For that reason, he wants to do something about his appearance. The first thing he will do is get rid of the wrinkles around his eyes and mouth. Then he will lose weight. He feels sensitive about being bald and plans to have a hair transplant. He doesn't like hairpieces. He is also going to get new dentures. He wears glasses because he doesn't see well, but he will get contact lenses. After he does all this, he will look younger. That's important in his business.

Let's Read about It

What to Do about Wrinkles

Wrinkled clothing is popular these days, but wrinkled skin is not. People, as they grow older, spend thousands of dollars each year on lotions, creams, make-up, treat-
5   ments, and surgery to get rid of wrinkles— those laugh lines around the mouth, crow's feet at the corners of the eyes, and worry lines on the forehead.

Anyone who lives long enough will
10 have wrinkles. With age, your skin loses its firmness and elasticity. If you want to know if your skin wrinkles easily, try this: Pinch some skin from the top of your hand, hold it for ten seconds, and then release it. If it
15 takes more than three seconds for the skin to bounce back into place, you are a wrinkler.

Vera Young, an expert on skin and ag-ing, says the most important factor in wrin-
20 kling is heredity—characteristics that you were born with. People with fair skin and light eyes wrinkle earlier than people with dark skin and dark eyes.

If you are a person who wrinkles easily, it is important to know the causes of wrin-   25 kling: sun, smoking, inactivity, dryness, and improper diet. Here are some do's and don't's of skin care as you grow older:

* Avoid the sun as much as possible. Wear sunglasses in the sun.   30

* Don't smoke. "A smoker's skin wrin-kles up to ten years sooner than a nonsmok-er's skin," says Ms. Young.

* Exercise. Inactivity allows wrinkles to form. Exercise puts more oxygen into the   35 skin and sweating removes impurities.

* Use a lotion or cream day and night and immediately after a bath. Drink six to eight glasses of water a day.

* Pay attention to your diet. Eat good   40 foods like dairy products, whole grains, and fresh fruits and vegetables.

EXERCISES

A. Match the following:

_____	1. wrinkling	a.	the skin's ability to bounce back
_____	2. exercise	b.	have more wrinkles
_____	3. smokers	c.	adds oxygen to the skin
_____	4. crow's feet	d.	a natural part of aging
_____	5. worry lines	e.	around the mouth
_____	6. laugh lines	f.	at the corners of the eyes
_____	7. elasticity	g.	above the eyes

B. Answer these questions.

1. What are crow's feet? Worry lines? Laugh lines? Where are they on the face?
2. Why is exercise good for the skin?
3. What are creams, lotions, treatments, and make-up used for?
4. Who gets wrinkles sooner?
5. What are ways to avoid wrinkles?
6. How can you test your skin's elasticity?
7. What role does heredity play in wrinkling?
8. How are dark-skinned people, nonsmokers, and active people similar?

UNIT 5

WHERE'S TWEETIE?

Let's Look at It

Do you have any pets?
If so, do they live in your house?
Do you ever worry about your pets?

Picture 1

Mr. and Mrs. Chin like animals a lot. As a matter of fact, they have four pets that live with them: a dog, a cat, a fish, and a bird named Tweetie. But something has happened to one of the pets.

VOCABULARY

A.   Answer these questions.
1.   What animals do you see in picture 1?
2.   What animals do you see in picture 2?

Picture 2

3. What animal is missing in picture 2?
4. What room is it?
5. What season of the year is it?

B. Match the following words and expressions.

_____	1.	canary	a. small outdoor place built into the wall of a building
_____	2.	cage	b. container for cut flowers
_____	3.	fireplace	c. a wire net in a window
_____	4.	balcony	d. a small bird
_____	5.	vase	e. an animal a person keeps in the house
_____	6.	mantel	f. a place in the house for burning wood
_____	7.	pet	g. a shelf on top of a fireplace
_____	8.	screen	h. an object in which a bird is kept

Let's Talk about It

A.   Compare the preceding pictures by completing these sentences.

1.   The cat is sleeping on the TV in picture 1, but in picture 2 . . .

2.   The bird is in the cage in picture 1, but . . .

3.   The dog is in the middle of the room in picture 1, but . . .

4.   The door to the cage is open a little in picture 1, but . . .

5.   Mr. Chin is not in the room in picture 1, but . . .

B.   Talk about these five possibilities with a partner. Why are they wrong?

1.   Maybe the bird flew out the window.
2.   Maybe the cat ate the bird.
3.   Maybe the dog ate the bird.
4.   Maybe the neighbors ate the bird for dinner.
5.   Maybe Mr. Chin let the bird out for air.

C.   Another possibility is not listed in exercise B. What do you think happened to Tweetie? Talk about this with members of your group.

Let's Write about It

A.   Write at least three things that didn't happen to Tweetie.

EXAMPLE: *He didn't fly out the window.*

1.   _____

2.   _____

3.   _____

B.   What happened to Tweetie? Finish the note Mr. Chin wrote to his wife before he went to work.

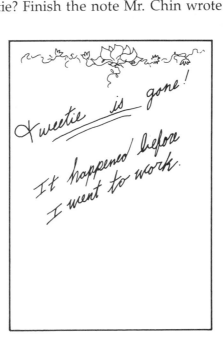

Tweetie is gone!

It happened before I went to work.

Let's Read about It

Pets and People

A wise person once said, "A dog is man's best friend." There is a lot of truth in this saying, for both women and men. Dogs and other pets are good for all people. Scientists now know that when you touch an animal lovingly, your blood pressure drops. Here are other benefits of having a pet that may surprise you.

● Patients who have pets recover more quickly after major surgery.

● Abused children learn to love again if they receive a pet.

● Violent prisoners become calm and peaceful when they care for pets.

● Old people and children who are silent and withdrawn become more expressive. They talk about their pets to anyone who will listen.

● Adults who had pets in childhood become more loving parents after they marry and have children.

People know a great deal about the benefits of having a pet, but we do not know how pets feel. Do they get the same benefits from people?

EXERCISES

A.   Find the words in the reading that mean the same as:

1. talkative   2. with affection   3. mistreated   4. not talkative   5. get better
6. using great force   7. advantages

B.   *True* or *false* or *I don't know?*

_____ 1.   Only dogs help people.

_____ 2.   Prisoners mistreat their pets.

_____ 3.   Pets help people to get well quickly from sickness.

_____ 4.   The blood pressure of a dog lowers if you pet it.

_____ 5.   People who do not have pets have poor health.

_____ 6.   Abused children also abuse their pets.

C.   Answer the following questions.

1.   Which other animals help people? How?
2.   Why do you think animals help people?

UNIT 6

GAMES PEOPLE PLAY

Let's Look at It

Do you have a favorite sport?
Which sports do you like to watch? To play?
Are you a good athlete?

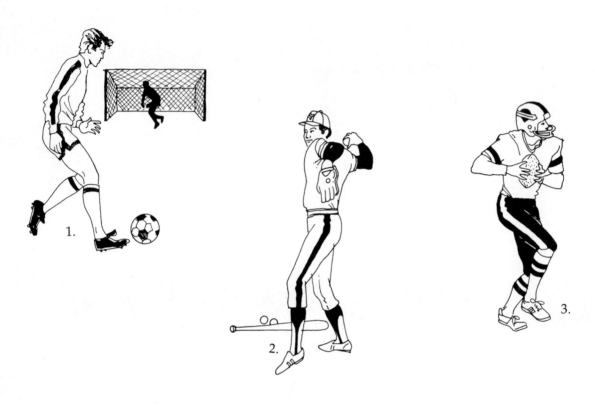

1.

2.

3.

4.

5.

6.

7.

8.

9.

10.

VOCABULARY

A.   Select the proper words to fill in the following blanks.

> ball   boxing   players   soccer   tennis
> smaller   points   field   score   teams

1.   Many of the sports require two _____ and many _____.

2.   Golf, soccer, and many other sports use a round _____.

3.   A golf ball is _____ than a _____ ball.

4.   Baseball and football players play on a _____.

5.   In many of the sports, the players earn _____, and the team or player with

 the higher _____ is the winner.

6.   Sports with only two players are _____ and _____.

B.   Do you know what these expressions mean and which sports they are from? Draw lines to match them.

1. Her report *touched all bases*.	a. usual, expected	football
2. It's a *toss-up*.	b. decided together	basketball
3. That's *par for the course*.	c. was complete	baseball
4. That's *hitting below the belt*.	d. undecided, unclear	tennis
5. They *went into a huddle* during the crisis.	e. You have to decide	boxing
6. *The ball is in your court*.	f. unfair, illegal	golf

Let's Talk about It

A.   Name each sport in the pictures on pages 46 and 47.

B.   Which of the sports

1.   Require two teams?
2.   Require two people?
3.   Require many people, not teams?
4.   Are usually played by men?

5.   Do women usually play?
6.   Are good for children?
7.   Are good for your health?
8.   Need a special playing area?

C.   In a small group compare the following sports. Discuss your reasons.

1.   *Boxing* or *ice hockey*: Which one is safer?
2.   *Football* or *auto racing*: Which one is more dangerous?
3.   *Soccer* or *baseball*: Which one is more exciting?
4.   *Golf* or *tennis*: Which one is easier to play?
5.   *Marathon racing* or *basketball*: Which one requires more training?
6.   *Baseball* or *basketball*: Which one requires more time to play?

D.   Answer the following questions and discuss your answers.

1.   Why do people play sports?
2.   Why do people watch sports?
3.   Who are some professional sports people? Why are they famous?
4.   Which sports do men and women play together?
5.   Why don't men and women play other sports together?
6.   Winning is very important in sports. Do you agree or disagree?

Courtesy of the METS

Marsha L. Botsford

E.   Look at the following information. Do you *agree* (A) or *disagree* (D) with the statements in the Opinion Survey? Discuss your answers.

Martina Navratilova—tennis player
Earnings: over $1 million last year

Kimberly Burr—nurse
Salary: $30,000 last year

Keith Hernandez—baseball player
Salary: about $1,650,000 last year

Isa Crasher—teacher
Salary: $28,000 last year

OPINION SURVEY

A D 1. Professional athletes make too much money.

A D 2. Teachers and nurses do not make enough money.

A D 3. Women athletes are not as good as men athletes.

A D 4. Men athletes are better than women athletes and deserve more money.

A D 5. The government needs to control the salaries of professional athletes.

A D 6. If athletes are able to get a lot of money, it's OK.

A D 7. Professional athletes are the best in their sports and deserve their high salaries.

A D 8. Professional athletes are good examples for young people.

F. Work with a partner and describe a sport that you know. Include the following information.

1. How many players are there?
2. Which positions do they play?
3. Where do they play?
4. What kind of equipment do they use?

5. How are points scored?
6. How many time periods are there?
7. How does a player or a team win?
8. How does the game begin and end?

Let's Write about It

A. Write your comparisons of these sports.

EXAMPLE: Tennis/golf: *Tennis is easier to play than golf.*

1. football/soccer: _____

_____

2. boxing/football: _____

_____

3. marathon racing/auto racing:_____

_____

4. baseball/basketball: _____

    _____

5. golf/tennis: _____

    _____

B. Write a paragraph about your favorite sport. Look again at the questions in exercise F (Let's Talk about It) and include the answers in your paragraph.

_____, My Favorite Sport

    _____

_____

_____

_____

_____

_____

_____

_____

_____

_____

Let's Read about It

Sports Violence

Some sports are violent. That's the nature of the game. Football and ice hockey are two examples. Players have to hit each other. Sometimes they get hurt. At a very early age, youngsters who play football or ice hockey learn to be tough and violent on the playing field. If they aren't, they don't become "good players."

Lately, however, there are reports of violence off the field, not by the players but by the "fans," the people who watch and support the teams. "Fan" comes from "fanatic," someone who is enthusiastic and unreasonable. In recent years many fans, especially soccer fans, have become very violent.

In 1985, 38 people were killed and 437 were injured at a soccer game between a British team and an Italian team in Brussels, Belgium. Some British fans attacked a few Italian fans sitting near them in the stadium. The police in the stadium were not able to control them. The outnumbered Italians were pressed against a brick wall that collapsed and buried them.

Another tragedy occurred in Sheffield, England in 1989. Ninety-five people were crushed to death when the police opened a gate, and a large crowd of fans rushed into the stadium. The fans who died were crushed against a steel fence next to the playing field.

The greatest violence at a soccer game occurred in Lima, Peru, in 1964. During a game between Peru and Argentina, there was a fight between the fans and, as a result, 318 people died.

Yet, the most serious conflict happened, not among the fans but between the armies of two countries. In 1969 the "futbol war" broke out at the border of El Salvador and Honduras among the soldiers posted there. These soldiers were fans of their national teams, and they were reacting to the results of a soccer game between the two countries. Who won? No one remembers now because it all seems so crazy.

Something is wrong. Violence by sports fans is destructive and unnecessary. After all, what is the purpose of sports? Isn't it to develop the body and the mind? Certainly. But there is also a need to encourage a sense of fair play instead of an overemphasis on winning. Win or lose, it doesn't matter. What matters really is *how* one plays the game. And when the game is over, to be humble as a winner and proud as a loser.

EXERCISES

A.   Look at the reading and find another way to say:

1.   supporter of a team
2.   not reasonable
3.   started
4.   physical force that injures
5.   rather than
6.   not believable
7.   happened
8.   fight between two groups
9.   fell down
10.   feeling unimportant
11.   unfortunate event

B.   Answer these questions.

1. In which sports are the players violent?
2. What happened in Brussels?
3. How was the "futbol war" different from other fan violence?
4. Where and when did the greatest loss of life occur?
5. What happened in Sheffield, England?
6. What do you think is the purpose of sports?
7. Why do you think sports fans become violent?

UNIT 7

SOMETHING'S BURNING

Let's Look at It

Have you eve seen a house on fire?
Have you ever had a fire in your house?
What would you take if your house were on fire?

VOCABULARY

A. In the picture find the room that contains the following items.

_____	1. jewelry	a. nursery
_____	2. wallet	b. garage
_____	3. baby	c. living room
_____	4. old pictures	d. study
_____	5. computer	e. bedroom
_____	6. computer disks	f. hall
_____	7. silver tea set	
_____	8. manuscript on computer disk	
_____	9. TV set	
_____	10. car	

B. Which of the items in the house *can you replace* and which *can't you replace*?

EXAMPLE: *You can replace the car, but you can't replace the old pictures.*

Let's Talk about It

A.   Decide which item in the following pairs is more important. Then compare your answers.

1. the wallet or the old pictures

EXAMPLE: *The old pictures are more important than the wallet.*

2. the baby or the car
3. the computer or the computer disks
4. the jewelry or the TV set
5. the computer or the tea set
6. the old pictures or the computer disks
7. the TV set or the silver tea set

B.   There's a fire in your house at night. What will you do? Number the following actions in order of importance (1 = most important, 9 = least important). Compare and discuss your answers with your classmates.

_____ 1. Look for the cat.

_____ 2. Call the fire department.

_____ 3. Put out the fire.

_____ 4. Take the children out of the house.

_____ 5. Wake up the other people in the house.

_____ 6. Take out the furniture.

_____ 7. Look for your wallet.

_____ 8. Get dressed.

_____ 9. Tell the neighbors.

C.   Your house is on fire. You can go into your house and bring out only what you can carry in one trip. Discuss with your group what you would save from the fire.

EXAMPLE: *If I could make one trip, I'd save _____ because _____.*

Let's Write about It

A. Write three sentences about what you *can replace* in your home.

1. _____

2. _____

3. _____

B. Write three sentences about what you *can't replace* in your home.

1. _____

2. _____

3. _____

C. Describe what is happening in the following pictures.

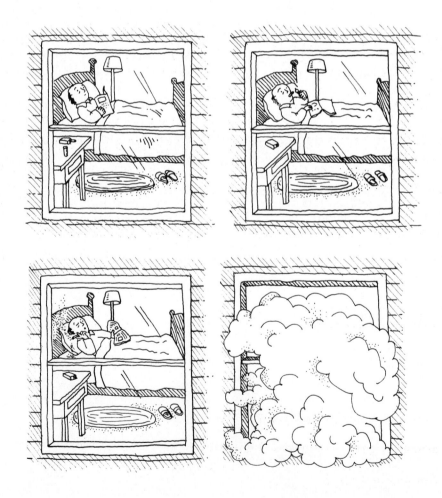

_____

_____

_____

_____

_____

_____

_____

Let's Read about It

Hot Crime

What is arson? It is the deliberate burning of property. Every year in the U.S. arson causes about one billion dollars worth of damage. There are many reasons why people, adults, and chil- (5) dren commit arson.

Adults usually set fires for profit or revenge. Owners of old buildings sometimes "torch" them to collect insurance money. They sometimes use the money to make repairs, but most often they (10) "pocket" the money and leave the property as it is. Other arsonists "burn out" people they dislike. They set fire to property to get even with someone.

The most surprising arsonists are children, (15) who set about 40 percent of the arson fires nation-wide. Some young children are curious about fire and like to watch it. Others like the excitement— the firefighters, the fire trucks, the sirens. Older children, often neglected by their parents, some- (20) times set fires because they feel a need for attention.

A few people have a psychological disorder called pyromania, an uncontrollable desire to start fires. These people are mentally ill and need (25) psychological help.

Arson is a serious crime. Property damage is just one of the results. The saddest result is that every year thousands of people are injured or die in unnecessary fires.

EXERCISES

A. Answer _true_ or _false_.

_____ 1. Arson fires start accidentally.

_____ 2. Some people make money from arson.

_____ 3. Arson is not illegal.

_____ 4. Children start many fires.

_____ 5. Pyromania is an illness.

_____ 6. Arson doesn't hurt anyone.

B. Complete the following sentences.

1. Neglected children sometimes start fires because _____.

2. Adults usually set fires because _____.

3. Very young children set fires because _____.

4. People who suffer from pyromania start fires because _____.

5. Arson affects all of us because _____.

UNIT 8

THE DOCTOR WILL SEE YOU NOW

Let's Look at It

What are some common health problems?
How often do you go to the doctor?
How can you stay healthy?

1.   2.   3.   4.

VOCABULARY

A.   Here are two different ways to say the same thing. Match them.

_____	1. She has a headache.	a. She has a temperature/fever.
_____	2. My stomach hurts.	b. She's expecting a baby.
_____	3. She feels hot.	c. I have a stomachache.
_____	4. He has a pain in his back.	d. He has chest pain.
_____	5. She's pregnant.	e. I've got a broken arm.
_____	6. His chest hurts.	f. Her head hurts.
_____	7. My arm's broken.	g. He's got a backache.

5.   6.   7.   8.

Let's Talk about It

A.   These patients are in the waiting room of the clinic. Which patient said each of the following sentences? Use the numbers to refer to the patients.

EXAMPLE: *Patient number one said, '' . . . . ''*

1.   "I was going up the stairs and my back snapped. I can't stand up straight."
2.   "I think it's time."
3.   "The other car didn't stop at the intersection and hit my car. I think my arm's broken."
4.   "This pain . . . It's in the upper part of my chest and it's running down my left arm."
5.   "Boy, do I have a headache! I've already taken four aspirins."
6.   "I was skiing. My body went one way, and my leg went another."
7.   "My stomach hurts. It's probably something I ate."
8.   "Ahhh . . . choo! Sniff. My nose is stopped up."

CARING TOUCH MEDICAL CENTER

420 Jamaica Avenue
Green Forest, NJ 00033
Telephone: 555-2978

Time	Patient's Name	Symptoms
5:02	Jeff Simpson	stomach pains
5:06	Bernice Lumsden	broken arm? facial scratches
5:09	Shinwon Kim	runny nose and fever
5:12	Linwood Lyons	back pain
5:14	Megan Rivera	headache
5:18	Helga Weiss	leg cast removal
5:19	Randolph Farnsworth	chest pain
5:20	Samantha Ferguson	pregnant

B. Answer these questions about the patients.

1. Who has the most serious problem?
2. Who has the least serious problem?
3. Who is in the clinic because of an accident?
4. Who seems to be in the most pain?
5. Who seems to be in the least pain?
6. Who doesn't really need to see a doctor?
7. Who needs to see a doctor immediately?
8. Who can probably come back another time?

C. Some of the patients have serious problems; others do not. The doctor should see the most serious cases first. With other students, discuss the patients and their problems and put them in the order that the doctor should see them. Give your reasons.

EXAMPLE: *The doctor should see* _____ *first because* _____.

D. What is your doctor like? Describe his or her (1) appearance, (2) manner with patients, and (3) office and equipment.

E. Circle A (*agree*) or D (*disagree*) for the following sentences. Then discuss your answers with your classmates..

OPINION SURVEY

A   D   1.   Doctors work long hours.

A   D   2.   Doctors make too much money.

A   D   3.   Medical care is too expensive in the United States.

A   D   4.   Patients trust doctors too much.

A   D   5.   Some people see their doctors too often.

A   D   6.   The government should pay for medical care.

A   D   7.   People should be able to watch after their own health.

A   D   8.   Doctors think they have all the answers.

A   D   9.   Female doctors are better than male doctors.

A   D   10. Doctors make patients wait too long.

Let's Write about It

A.   Write the order in which the doctor should see the patients and give the reason.

EXAMPLE: *The doctor should see* _____ *first because* _____.

1. _____

2. _____

3. _____

4. _____

5. _____

6. _____

7. _____

8. _____

B.   Finish the report that the nurse started on the next page. Write the patients' names and their health problems in the order the doctor saw them.

C.   Write a short paragraph describing your doctor. Use your ideas from exercise D.

_____

_____

_____

_____

_____

CARING TOUCH MEDICAL CENTER

This afternoon the clinic was very busy. Our first patient was

Let's Read about It

Read this story. Choose the correct word in parentheses that fits.

The Psychiatric Appointment

It took Mrs. Doby a long (day, night, time), but at last her husband agreed to see a psychiatrist. The conversation went like this.

"Doctor Fromd, you (sincerely, simply, quickly) must do something about my (husband, problem, health)," the worried woman said.

5 "Well, Mrs. Doby, what seems to be the (wrong, matter, story) with your husband?" the doctor asked sympathetically.

"There's nothing (wrong, correct, matter) with me," Mr. Doby interrupted. "You should really have a look at (myself, my wife, my throat)."

"Now honey," she said, "There's nothing to (be done, talk about, be ashamed of)." Mrs. Doby

10 spoke gently to her husband. Then she turned to the doctor. "You (look, see, hear), Doctor, he thinks he's a refrigerator."

"Oh, Gladys, honestly!" harrumphed Mr. Doby impatiently.

"A refrigerator? Well, I don't see anything so (good, simple, bad) about that. It certainly isn't harmful, (does it, isn't it, is it)?"

15 "Not to *him* maybe. But it sure (pleases, bothers, understands) me," Mrs. Doby answered.

"(Maybe, Exactly, Surely) how does that bother you, Mrs. Doby?" the doctor asked.

"It keeps me (asleep, awake, worried)."

Dr. Fromd stopped (listening, looking, talking) for a while. He thought about the situation: This woman says that her husband thinks he's a refrigerator. It's not a problem for (her, him, them), but it *is*

20 a problem for (him, her, them). He continued a little puzzled.

"Just (when, how, where) does that keep you awake, Mrs. Doby?" asked the doctor.

"It's (quite, very much, a lot) simple really," Mrs. Doby explained. "My husband always sleeps with his mouth open."

"Umm huh," hummed the doctor in his most understanding manner.

25 ". . . and the light keeps me awake."

EXERCISES

A.   Who in the story is worried? sympathetic? awake? impatient? puzzled? sick?

B.   Answer these questions.

1.   What is funny about this story?
2.   Who really has a problem?
3.   Why do you think Mr. Doby agreed to see Dr. Fromd?
4.   What do you think Dr. Fromd will do?
5.   Do you know anyone like Mrs. Doby?
6.   How can Dr. Fromd help Mr. and Mrs. Doby?

UNIT 9

WHO TOOK THE TIARA?

Let's Look at It

Do you like to have expensive jewelry?
Why do people like jewelry?
What are the risks of having jewelry?

Prince Igor

Princess Rina

Virgil Yesserie, The Prince's Butler

Harvey Featherbrane, The Chauffeur

Sir Avery Slikenfast, The Ambassador

Millicent Merriweather, The Princess's Maid

Ingrid Fairbottom, The Royal Couple's Press Secretary

Princess's Tiara Stolen

City police report that a valuable tiara is missing. It belongs to Princess Rina, who is visiting the city with her husband Prince Igor. The diamond and emerald tiara, worth over a million dollars, was taken sometime last night from the royal suite at the Dorchester Hotel, where the prince and princess are staying. The police suspect that the tiara was stolen by someone close to the royal couple. There are several suspects. The investigation is continuing under Detective Marcel Oiseau.

VOCABULARY

A.   Match the following words with their meanings.

_____	1. expensive	a.	finding information about a crime
_____	2. missing	b.	set of rooms in a hotel
_____	3. tiara	c.	very hard clear stone
_____	4. diamond	d.	cannot be found
_____	5. emerald	e.	valuable
_____	6. suite	f.	go on without stopping
_____	7. royal	g.	valuable green stone
_____	8. investigation	h.	related to a king or queen
_____	9. continue	i.	small crown

B.   *True* or *false*?

_____   1.   The tiara was lost.

_____   2.   A stranger probably stole the tiara.

_____   3.   The princess was wearing the tiara.

_____   4.   The stones in the tiara are clear and green.

_____   5.   The tiara is worth less than $1,000,000.

_____   6.   The police know who stole the tiara.

Let's Talk about It

A.   Answer these questions.

1.   Where are the prince and princess staying?
2.   What is the value of the tiara?

3. What kinds of precious stones are in the tiara?
4. What do the police think about the theft?
5. How many people are in the royal couple's group?

B. Work with a partner. Describe one of the following persons. (What does he or she look like? What is he or she wearing?) Do not give the name. Have your partner guess the name. Then your partner describes one of the people and you guess the name.

Princess Rina   Prince Igor   Harvey Fetherbrane   Virgil Yesserie

Millicent Merriweather   Ingrid Fairbottom   Sir Avery Slikenfast

C. The famous detective Marcel Oiseau is ready to solve the mystery of the stolen tiara. Here are his clues:

- He found a long black hair near where the tiara was.
- He noticed a strong smell of expensive floral perfume in the room.
- He saw a skin rash on the maid's neck.
- He knew that the prince and the princess, two men, and a women were at a press conference at the embassy.
- He smelled the scent of Bouquet, a very expensive perfume, when he interviewed the press secretary.
- One of the servants doesn't usually wear perfume because of an allergy.
- A witness saw the servant who doesn't have long hair reading in the lobby of the hotel.
- Detective Oiseau knows that some of these clues are real, but others are misleading.

Answer these questions based on Detective Oiseau's information.

1. Where was the butler? The ambassador? The prince? The princess? The press secretary? The maid? The chauffeur?
2. Was the thief wearing expensive floral perfume? Where do you think the thief got the perfume.
3. Only one person was able to steal the tiara. Who is that person?
4. Which clues did the thief leave to point to someone else?
5. Which clues point to the real thief?
6. Who *couldn't have* or *could have* stolen the tiara? Give reasons.

Let's Write about It

A. Who *couldn't have* stolen the tiara and why? Write your answers.

1. _____

2. _____

3. _____

4. _____

5. _____

6. _____

Who *could have* stolen the tiara? Why?

7. _____

B. Write a newspaper report of the theft. Tell what happened, when and where it happened, and who was involved.

_____

_____

_____

_____

_____

Let's Read about It

A status symbol is something that makes you appear rich or successful. Match the following advertisements with the pictures of each status symbol.

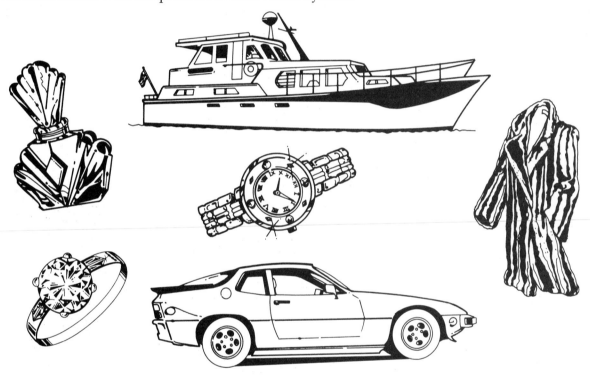

1. Come in from the cold. Wrap yourself in warm elegance this winter. Enjoy the comfort of fur.
2. For centuries kings and queens have worn precious stones. Now you can be a princess with this beautifully cut gem set in solid gold. It's one of nature's rarest creations—with more fire and sparkle.
3. Perfect for entertaining or business meetings, your 104-foot castle on the water can take you around the harbor or around the world.
4. It doesn't just tell you the time. It tells you something about yourself. A unique timepiece of elegance, accuracy, and rare perfection.
5. Your presence will remain long after you with this exotic blend of fragrances. For the sophisticated woman who wants to be remembered.
6. Curving softly like a well-muscled animal, its fluid shape and comfortable interior say this is a vehicle of uncommon luxury. In motion, it is a perfect balance between sports handling and smooth ride.

EXERCISES

A.   Match the status symbols with the key words from the advertisements.

_____ 1.	boat	A. handling	G. accuracy	M. ride
_____ 2.	watch	B. sparkle	H. fragrance	N. fire
_____ 3.	fur coat	C. blend	I. wrap	O. gold
_____ 4.	perfume	D. harbor	J. vehicle	P. stone
_____ 5.	car	E. timepiece	K. water	Q. winter
_____ 6.	diamond ring	F. warm	L. remain	

B.   In your opinion, which words help to sell each status symbol? What does each product offer to the buyer?

UNIT 10

JACKPOT!

Let's Look at It

Do you watch game shows on television?
Which game shows do you watch?
What would you buy if you won money on a game show?

VOCABULARY

A. Put the following words in the correct column:

a) FURNITURE   b) CLOTHES   c) APPLIANCES

_____   _____   _____

_____   _____   _____

_____   _____   _____

1. fur coat   6. dress
2. refrigerator 7. stove
3. TV set   8. desk
4. table   9. chairs
5. pants

B. Here are two different ways to say the same thing. Match them.

_____	1. hit the jackpot	a. graduate from school
_____	2. go on a tour	b. watch a game show
_____	3. attend your commencement	c. take a vacation
_____	4. purchase a motor vehicle	d. win a big prize
_____	5. view a contest	e. buy a car

Let's Talk about It

A. Deborah can buy any of the items in the pictures.
What would you buy if you were Deborah?
EXAMPLE: *If I were Deborah, I'd buy a house.*

B. What are some other things you could do with this money?
EXAMPLE: *I could give some to the poor.*

C. How would you spend the $100,000?
Write the amounts in the following blanks. Then compare and discuss your answers.

$_____ savings account	$_____ your family or friends
$_____ charities for the poor	$_____ new clothes
$_____ education	$_____ new furniture/appliances
$_____ a new car	$_____ a vacation
$_____ a religious organization	$_____ bills
$_____ a new house or apartment	$_____ other _____

D. Circle A (*agree*) or D (*disagree*) for the following sentences. Then discuss your answers with a partner.

OPINION SURVEY

A D 1. Money brings happiness.

A D 2. It's better to give than to receive.

A D 3. People become rich by working hard.

A D 4. I like to buy new things.

A D 5. People should share what they have.

A D 6. Education is the most important thing in life.

A D 7. We remember people for the good things they do.

Let's Write about It

A. Complete the following sentences.

1. If I won $100,000 dollars, I would _____.

2. If I were younger, _____.

3. If I were older, _____.

4. If I lost my house keys, _____.

5. If I could change something in the world, _____.

6. If I could change something about myself, _____.

B.   Write the story of what happened in the pictures. Give the story a title.

_____

_____

_____

_____

_____

_____

_____

_____

_____

_____

_____

_____

_____

_____

_____

Let's Read about It

There's Always a Winner

Game shows are among the most popular programs on television. A game show has contestants (the people who play the game) and the host (the person who tells the contestants what to do). The contestants try to win money and prizes. There is always a winner and a loser on a TV game show. That is what makes them so attractive to the audience at home.

There are several types of TV game shows: (1) word games, where the contestants fill in missing letters to form words or phrases; (2) quizzes, where the contestants answer questions about history, science, music, and so on; and (3) guessing games, the contestants guess the price of various prizes or what others have said or think. Some of these games require skill or knowledge while others depend on luck and chance. The rules of the game are always simple and easy to understand.

For thirty years, TV game shows have been pretty much the same, but soon things will change. Some TV producers are now suggesting games that allow viewer participation at home. By getting game cards from the TV station, home audiences will be able to play the game along with the contestants in the TV studio. Viewers will be able to win cash and prizes right in their own homes.

EXERCISES

A. Match the following:

_____	1.	new game	a.	tells what to do
_____	2.	contestant	b.	fill in missing letters
_____	3.	word game	c.	answer questions
_____	4.	quiz	d.	give prices of prizes
_____	5.	host	e.	play at home
_____	6.	guessing game	f.	plays the game

B. Answer the following questions.

1. How will TV game shows change in the future?
2. What are the three different types of TV game shows?
3. Why does every TV game show have a host?
4. What always happens on a TV game show?
5. Why do people play TV game shows?
6. Why do people watch TV game shows?

UNIT 11

WHO'S WINNING

Let's Look at It

Do you ever gamble?
Are you a "lucky" or "unlucky" person?
Have you ever won anything?

Name: Rob Whitcomb
Marital status: divorced
Occupation: retired gardener
Age: 65
Education: finished high school
Gambling record: lost $40 after playing
                     the slot machine

Comments: "I always lose. I've never won anything."

Name: Ella Gamberg
Marital status: widowed
Occupation: bus driver
Age: 55
Education: dropped out of high school
Gambling record: lost $750 playing roulette

Comments: "I'll be back next month. I'm sure my luck will change."

Name: Jonah Greene
Marital status: single
Occupation: accountant
Age: 25
Education: finished college
Gambling record: Won $200 betting on
                     a boxing match

Comments: "I got lucky tonight. I think I'll leave while I'm ahead."

Name: Rita Ortega
Marital status: married
Occupation: computer programmer
Age: 40
Education: finished college
Gambling record: lost $1,300 playing
                     blackjack

Comments: "It doesn't matter. I had a lot of fun. I'm sure I'll win it all back sooner or later."

VOCABULARY

A.   Match the words with their meanings.

_____	1.	gamble	a.	a person who plays games for money
_____	2.	casino	b.	to play games for money
_____	3.	gambler	c.	having a feeling that one will win
_____	4.	win	d.	a building where people play games for money
_____	5.	lucky	e.	the practice of playing games for money
_____	6.	gambling	f.	money taken in (in gambling)
_____	7.	winnings	g.	to receive money as a result of success or luck in a game
_____	8.	lose	h.	to take a chance
_____	9.	bet	i.	to pay money on a game in the hope of getting more money back
_____	10.	risk	j.	to fail to win

B.   The words in parentheses in the following paragraph are not in the correct places. Rearrange them so that they are in their correct places.

These four people are (1) (bets)   . They love to (2) (won)   their money by making (3) (gamblers)   . They like to go to (4) (sports)   , where they can play different games of chance. Mrs. Gamberg likes to play (5) (blackjack)   , but Mrs. Ortega prefers (6) (roulette)   . Mr. Whitcomb likes to take his chances against the "one-armed bandits," the (7) (casinos)   . All three people are (8) (lucky)   . However, Mr. Greene bets on (9) (slot machine)   events, and he recently (10) (risk) $200 on a boxing match. Right now he feels (11) (unlucky)   . (12) (winning)   is their hobby, even if they know the casinos are (13) (gambling)   more than they are.

Let's Talk about It

A.   Match the following:

_____	1. Rob Whitcomb	a.	a sports event
_____	2. Ella Gamberg	b.	feels negative about gambling
_____	3. Jonah Greene	c.	a card game
_____	4. Rita Ortega	d.	doesn't work
		e.	roulette
		f.	never married
		g.	lost the most money
		h.	slot machine
		i.	probably gambles regularly
		j.	has the most education
		k.	was lucky
		l.	was unlucky

B.   Answer the following questions about the winnings of six casinos in Atlantic City.

WINNINGS OF SIX CASINOS IN ATLANTIC CITY (last six months)	
Bally's Casino	$114 million
Caesar's Casino	$110 million
Trump Palace Casino	$118.4 million
Harrah's Casino	$102.6 million
Resorts International Casino	$122.9 million
Tropicana Casino	$110.6 million

1.   Which casino had the most winnings? The least?
2.   How much do you think Caesar's will win for the entire year? What about the other casinos?
3.   Two casinos won about the same. Which are they?
4.   Why do you think some casinos have more winnings than others?
5.   Which casino would you want to go to if you were a gambler?

6. If you were a casino owner, which casino would you like to own?
7. Which forms of gambling do you think these casinos have?
8. If the casinos made this money as profit, how much do you think they paid out to gamblers?

C. Circle A (*agree*) or D (*disagree*) for the following sentences. Compare and discuss your answers.

OPINION SURVEY

A   D   1.   Gamblers have a lot of money.

A   D   2.   Most people get rich gambling.

A   D   3.   Gamblers are usually unhappy.

A   D   4.   Gambling is simply a matter of luck.

A   D   5.   A good gambler is skillful.

A   D   6.   Gambling is a problem for some people.

A   D   7.   Gambling causes a lot of crime.

A   D   8.   Most good gamblers are men.

D. In a group discuss your answers to these questions.

1. You probably know other ways of gambling. Explain them. Which of these would a serious gambler bet on? Which of these would an occasional gambler bet on?
2. Have you ever gambled? If so, how? If not, why not?
3. Some people gamble regularly. Why do you think they do this? Do you think they have a problem?
4. Some people dream of winning a lot of money. Is this a good attitude to have?
5. Who are the real winners in gambling?
6. What is your opinion about gambling?

Let's Write about It

A.   Look at the list of casinos. Rewrite the list according to the amount of the winnings (the highest, second highest, the least, and so on).

EXAMPLE: *Resorts International Casino, with over $122 million in winnings in the last six months, had the highest winnings in Atlantic City.*

1. _____

_____

2. _____

_____

3. _____

_____

4. _____

_____

5. _____

_____

B.   Write down the feelings of these people.

EXAMPLE: Rob Whitcomb: *He says that he always loses.*

1. Ella Gamberg: _____

2. Rita Ortega: _____

3. Jonah Greene: _____

4. Rob Whitcomb: _____

C. Write a paragraph by answering the following questions. In your answers use complete sentences and the words in parentheses.

The Real Winners

1. Who are the big winners in casino gambling? (. . . really . . .)
2. How much do the casinos in Atlantic City win each year? (In fact, . . .)
3. Do the gamblers win much money? (By comparison, . . . not . . . at all.)
4. Do they continue to gamble? (However, . . .) Why do they continue to gamble (. . . because . . .)

_____

_____

_____

_____

_____

_____

Let's Read about It

Help for Problem Gamblers

Some people have a problem with gambling. Like alcoholics who cannot control themselves, their problem is psychological. Jake Starnes—that is not his real name—has
5   such a problem.

"Whenever I had a dollar in my pocket, I went to the casino," he said recently, "Sometimes I won, and when I did, I was on top of the world. But most of the time, I lost.
10 I bet on horse races, played cards, roulette— any way to win.

"The problem was I rarely won. I borrowed money from my family. I told them I needed it. I didn't pay my bills. I gambled. It
15 wasn't a game anymore. I didn't control it. It controlled me. I almost lost everything I had."

Just as there are special organizations for problem drinkers, such as Alcoholics Anonymous (AA), there are similar organiza- 20 tions for problem gamblers. Many habitual gamblers need special psychological help, and Gamblers Anonymous (GA) is an organization that gives this help. Jake is a member.

Through GA, problem gamblers can 25 talk to other people with the same problem. They understand each other. When a gambler has the temptation to gamble, he or she can talk about it with someone who can help. The gambler is no longer alone with 30 the problem. It is shared. "Without GA," says Jake Starnes, "I would be in the street. Now I am ready to help others with a gambling problem."

EXERCISES

A. Find the words or expressions that mean the following.

1. felt wonderful (paragraph 2)
2. with the name not known (4)
3. done regularly, sometimes with harm (4)
4. something that strongly attracts or pulls you (5)
5. divided with others (5)

B. *True* or *false.*

_____ 1. Jake Starnes has a drinking problem.

_____ 2. GA and AA help people with psychological problems.

_____ 3. We don't know Starnes's real name.

_____ 4. Jake Starnes still has a gambling problem.

_____ 5. He only made small gambling bets.

_____ 6. Starnes went to a psychiatrist.

C. Answer these questions.

1. What other group with a problem is mentioned? What is the problem of members of that group?
2. How does GA work? How does it help problem gamblers?
3. What are some of the things Starnes did as a gambler?
4. When people with the same problem talk, they can help each other. Why is this true? Name other problems that people have where this is true.

UNIT 12

THE BROKEN WINDOW

Let's Look at It

What is a burglary?
Do burglaries happen in your country?
Has your home ever been burglarized?

There was a burglar in Gracie Blum's apartment. She is talking to Harold, the doorman, about it.

GRACIE: Harold, someone broke into my apartment. Did you see any strangers in the building today?

HAROLD: Oh, no! This morning I saw a woman wearing a fur coat. She rushed out the door and got into a waiting car. At first, I thought it was you, Miss Blum.

GRACIE: Wearing a fur coat? But it's not cold.

HAROLD: I know. The coat was buttoned up tightly, though.

GRACIE: That was probably the burglar, Harold. The police are on their way.

VOCABULARY

A. Match the following.

———	1. a thief who steals from houses or apartments	a. break into
———	2. the act of breaking into a house or an apartment	b. burglar
———	3. cloth covering for a floor	c. fur coat
———	4. a garment made from animal skin	d. burglary
———	5. enter a place forcefully	e. buttoned up tightly
———	6. closed firmly	f. carpet

B. Underline the things in the first picture of the apartment. Circle the things that are missing in the second picture.

fur coat computer typewriter watch records carpet bed desk plant coffee pot cup plate money clothing stereo bracelet chair necklace radio table ring clock statue

Let's Talk about It

A. Match the following:

_____	1.	burglar's possible manner of dress	a.	window and pot
_____	2.	a stolen object	b.	coffee and cake
_____	3.	a possible witness	c.	buttoned fur coat
_____	4.	the victim	d.	not long after Gracie left
_____	5.	clues to the criminal's sex	e.	a valuable carpet
_____	6.	the time of the burglary	f.	Harold, the doorman
_____	7.	the burglar's food	g.	lipstick and footprints
_____	8.	broken objects	h.	Gracie Blum

B. What do you know about this burglary? Discuss your answers. Use these symbols:

+   if you are sure it's true

?   if you aren't sure

/   if you think it is probable

-   if you know it's false

The burglar

_____ 1. entered through the window

_____ 2. turned over the plant accidentally

_____ 3. was looking for something special

_____ 4. is a woman

_____ 5. entered through the door

_____ 6. took something very valuable

_____ 7. left through the window

_____ 8. broke the window from the outside

_____ 9. entered the apartment in the morning

_____10. left through the door

_____11. knew the doorman

_____12. and the doorman were working together

C. With a partner, talk about the differences between the two pictures.

EXAMPLE: *There's a carpet in the first picture, but there isn't one in the second picture.*

D. Answer these questions about the burglary. Discuss your answers with your classmates. Say what *clearly* or *probably* happened.

1. How did the burglar enter and leave the apartment?
2. What do you know about the burglar?
3. What did the burglar eat and drink?

4. Where did the burglar look? Why?
5. What did the burglar break? Why?
6. What do the footprints show about the burglary?
7. When was the burglary? How do you know?
8. Did the burglar work alone? How do you know?
9. What did the burglar steal? How? Why?
10. How does Gracie Blum feel?

E. Look at the things in Gracie Blum's apartment. Which object(s) is (are)

1. the most valuable?
2. for entertainment?
3. need electricity?
4. easiest to sell?
5. most difficult to sell?

6. the easiest to carry?
7. the most difficult to carry?
8. possessions of rich people?
9. require an expert to know the true value?
10. decorative? functional?

Let's Write about It

A. Write three things that *probably* happened during the burglary.
EXAMPLE: *The burglar probably entered through the window.*

1. _____

2. _____

3. _____

B. Write three things that *clearly* happened during the burglary.
EXAMPLE: *It is clear that the burglar broke the window.*

1. _____

2. _____

3. _____

C. Finish this report that the doorman started.

AMAZON ARMS APARTMENTS

378 Richland Avenue

Chapelmont, VA 22245

Around 9:30 this morning, a burglar broke into Miss Blum's apartment. It seems clear that the burglar was a woman. She...

Let's Read about It

How to Prevent a Burglary

Burglary is increasing. Do not let yourself become a victim of this crime. Here are some suggestions that can make it difficult for a burglar to enter your home.

1. Install good, strong locks on doors that lead to the outside. The doors should be strong and solid. Most burglars enter through doors.
2. Put metal bars over any windows so a burglar cannot get through. The bars do not have to look like a prison. You can make them decorative as well as strong.
3. If there are a lot of burglaries in your neighborhood, install a burglar alarm. Some of the new electronic alarms detect noise, movement, or heat. Some can even telephone the police—all automatically. And, best of all, they are easy to install and not too expensive.
4. Get to know your neighbors well. They can keep an eye on your home, and you can do the same for them when they are away.
5. If you are going to be away for a few days or longer,
   - stop the delivery of the newspaper;
   - ask someone to pick up your mail every day;
   - install an answering machine on your telephone. (Do not say that you are away; ask the caller to leave a message and you will call back.)

If you ever see a burglary in progress, do not try to stop it yourself. Call the police immediately. Remember burglars are law breakers, and, like other criminals, they are dangerous.

EXERCISES

A.   Choose the correct answer.

1. You cannot prevent a burglary by (a) changing locks, (b) installing bars, (c) going away for a few days, (d) getting to know your neighbors.
2. When you are away, you should *not* (a) have someone pick up your mail, (b) leave a message on your answering machine, (c) stop the newspaper, (d) leave a note on the door.
3. If you see a burglary, (a) call your neighbor immediately, (b) call the police, (c) try to stop the burglar, (d) ask the burglar for identification.
4. Which is *not* true about new burglar alarms? They (a) are very expensive, (b) are electronic, (c) detect noise, (d) detect heat.
5. "Remember, burglars are law breakers" means they are (a) people, (b) careless, (c) forgetful, (d) dangerous.
6. Most burglars (a) go through windows, (b) enter through doors, (c) take small valuable objects, (d) are criminals.

B.   Answer these questions.

1.   To prevent a burglary, what can you do to the outside doors? To the windows? With your neighbors?
2.   If you are going to be away, what can you do about the newspaper? About the mail? About the telephone?
3.   If there are a lot of burglaries in your neighborhood, what can you do?
4.   What are the new burglar alarms like?
5.   If you see a burglary, what should you do?
6.   Which of these suggestions can Gracie Blum use?

UNIT 13

UNDER THE

TABLE

Let's Look at It

What is bribery?
Is bribery common in your country?
What do you think "under the table" means?

Mr. Lupo: How did I do?

Officer Hill: Not that well, Mr. Lupo.

Mr. Lupo: But I have to pass. I need a driver's license. What can I do?

Officer Hill: I'm afraid you . . .

Mr. Lupo: Listen, here's a hundred dollars. Can't you help me?

Officer Hill: I'll see what I can do.

Mr. Jones: You're getting an F for the course, you know, Luke.

Luke: But that means I won't graduate, Mr. Jones.

Mr. Jones: I'm really sorry about that, Luke.

Luke: Here take my watch, Mr. Jones. You can have it. But, please, Mr. Jones. Let me pass so I can graduate with my friends.

Mr. Jones: Luke, are you trying to bribe me?

Ms. Leroy: Your company makes very good computer software.

Ms. Fletcher: Then we'll get the government contract?

Ms. Leroy: I didn't say that, but I think I can arrange it.

Ms. Fletcher: You know, this contract is very important to me.

Ms. Leroy: How important *is* it to you, Ms. Fletcher?

Ms. Fletcher: I think this envelope shows you how important it is.

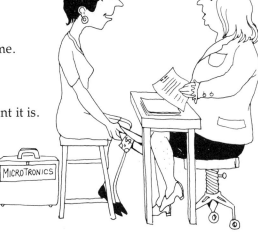

VOCABULARY

A.   Find the word or expression that has the same meaning:

1. permit to drive a car
2. I'm not going to finish school
3. to give an illegal gift
4. "thinking" machine
5. make something happen

B.   Match the following:

_____	1. Mr. Jones, the teacher	a.	took a bribe
_____	2. Ms. Leroy, the supervisor	b.	failed the course
_____	3. Mr. Lupo, the driver	c.	didn't take a bribe
_____	4. Ms. Fletcher, the salesperson	d.	failed the road test
_____	5. Luke, the student	e.	works for the government
_____	6. Officer Hill, the driver's license examiner	f.	sells computer software
		g.	gave a bribe

C.   Answer the following questions.

1. What is a road test?
2. How much did the driver pay to "pass" the road test?
3. What can Officer Hill do?
4. Why does Luke offer Mr. Jones his watch?
5. Why is Luke so upset about the grade?
6. Who sells very good computer software?
7. Why is Ms. Fletcher speaking with Ms. Leroy?
8. What does Ms. Fletcher want?
9. What can Ms. Leroy arrange?
10. Who are the bribe givers in these situations? The bribe takers?

Let's Talk about It

A.   *True* or *false* or *I don't know*? Discuss your answer with a partner.

_____   1.   If Ms. Fletcher pays the bribe, she will be happy.

_____   2.   If she pays the bribe, she will feel guilty.

_____   3.   If she pays the bribe, she will go to jail.

_____   4.   If she doesn't pay the bribe, she will get the contract anyway.

_____   5.   If she doesn't pay the bribe, her company will go out of business.

_____   6.   If she doesn't pay the bribe, she can report Ms. Leroy to the police or to her superiors.

B. Look at the picture on page 108. Discuss what Ms. Fletcher thinks.

1. What are some "good" things that Ms. Fletcher imagines if she pays the bribe? (See 1)
2. What are some bad things that she imagines if she pays the bribe? (See 2)
3. What might happen if she pays the bribe? (See 4)
4. What might happen if she doesn't pay the bribe? (See 3)
5. What can Ms. Fletcher do about Ms. Leroy?

C. In a small group decide what each person in each situation should do. Discuss your different opinions and come to an agreement. Remember to listen to and consider the opinions of others. Use *should* or *shouldn't* and give reasons (*because*).

1. What should Officer Hill do?
2. What should Mr. Jones do?
3. What should Ms. Fletcher do?
4. What would you do in each situation if you were Mr. Lupo? if you were Officer Hill? if you were Luke? if you were Mr. Jones? if you were Ms. Fletcher? if you were Ms. Leroy?

D.   Circle A (*agree*) or D (*disagree*) for the following statements. Then compare and discuss your answers with a partner.

OPINION SURVEY

A   D   1. Sometimes you have to "pay" a bribe to succeed.

A   D   2. It's okay to give a teacher or a boss a gift.

A   D   3. Bribes make life easier.

A   D   4. Bribery, like robbery, is a serious crime.

A   D   5. People who give or take bribes are usually caught.

A   D   6. A bribe doesn't really harm anyone if no one says anything.

A   D   7. Government employees take bribes because they are underpaid.

A   D   8. There is no difference between bribes and gifts or tips.

A   D   9. Most people are really honest.

A   D   10. Most bribe takers are greedy people.

Let's Write about It

A.   Write two things that *will probably* happen if Ms. Fletcher pays the bribe.
EXAMPLE: *If she pays the bribe, she will probably get the contract.*

1. _____

2. _____

B.   Write three things that *will probably* happen if Ms. Fletcher doesn't pay the bribe.
EXAMPLE: If she doesn't pay the bribe, she probably won't get the contract.

1. _____

2. _____

3. _____

C.   Take the role of Officer Hill, Mr. Jones, or Ms. Fletcher. Write what happened from that person's point of view. Write the paragraph in the first person ("I"). Give your paragraph a title.

_____

_____

_____

_____

_____

_____

_____

_____

_____

_____

_____

Let's Read about It

No More Bribes

Bribery is an ancient practice. Giving money or gifts to people in positions to help you was a common practice in the United States, at least until the twentieth century. It was once pos-

5 sible to bribe government officials without fear of punishment. High government officials and judges were the only exceptions. Bribing a judge has always been a serious crime. Some say bribery is still common in the United States, but now

10 bribe givers and takers are more careful. They do not want a public scandal. Nothing sells newspapers and magazines better than a good bribery scandal.

Today in the United States most people be-

15 lieve that it is dishonest to give or take a bribe. This view means that you cannot give a "gift" to a government official or a manager in a company in exchange for special favors. The disapproval of bribery comes from the belief that all people de-

20 serve fair and equal treatment ("fair play"). When you bribe someone, you are trying to "buy" unfair advantage, which other people do not have. The punishment for bribery ranges from heavy fines to imprisonment, or both.

25 Although bribery is illegal in most countries, it still exists in varying degrees all over the world. Recent international scandals involved bribery in selling jet planes, weapons, and oil. In some countries it is nearly impossible to get any-

30 thing done without first paying a bribe. In other countries bribe takers and bribe givers are punished severely.

Which is worse: to give a bribe or to take one? Do we avoid bribery because we are so hon-

35 est? Or is it our sense of "fair play" that keeps us honest? Or are we simply afraid of being caught?

EXERCISES

A. Answer *true* or *false* or *I don't know*.

_____ 1. Bribery is wrong, but not illegal.

_____ 2. Bribery is an old practice but is decreasing now.

_____ 3. Two hundred years ago people didn't give bribes.

_____ 4. If you take a bribe, you can go to prison.

_____ 5. People all over the world give and take bribes.

_____ 6. In some countries there is nothing wrong with bribing government officials.

_____ 7. In the United States it is illegal to bribe judges.

_____ 8. Bribes give unfair advantage to the bribe taker.

_____ 9. Different countries see bribery in different ways.

_____ 10. Bribery does not allow for "fair play."

B. Complete the following sentences.

1. Bribery is _____.

2. One gives a bribe in exchange for _____.

3. _____ ranges from heavy fines to imprisonment.

4. In some countries _____ to get anything done.

5. All people deserve _____.

6. Today Americans think _____.

7. Recent international bribery involved _____.

8. Bribery is wrong because _____.

UNIT 14

ALL AROUND US

Let's Look at It

What kinds of pollution are there?
How does pollution happen?
What can we do to prevent pollution?

1a Then

1b Now

2a Then

2b Now

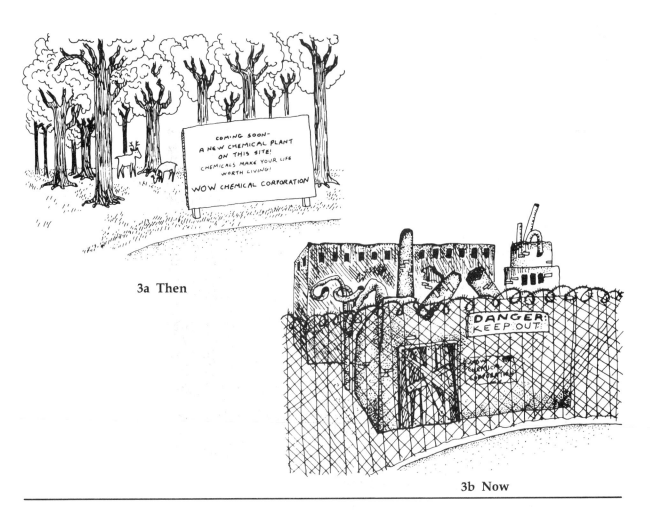

3a Then

3b Now

4a Then

4b Now

VOCABULARY

A. Without looking back, match the pictures and the following words:

WORDS

_____1. beach	_____ 9. seashells	1a
_____2. meadow	_____10. flowers	1b
_____3. chemical plant	_____11. garbage dump	2a
_____4. forest	_____12. ocean	2b
_____5. birds	_____13. smoke	3a
_____6. trucks	_____14. airplane	3b
_____7. oil refinery	_____15. marshland	4a
_____8. airport	_____16. noise	4b

B. Match the following:

CAUSE OF POLLUTION

_____ 1. airplanes
_____ 2. cars
_____ 3. chemicals
_____ 4. garbage
_____ 5. factories
_____ 6. trucks and buses
_____ 7. people
_____ 8. oil

KIND OF POLLUTION

a. water pollution
b. land pollution
c. noise pollution
d. air pollution

Let's Talk about It

A. Which choice is more important, a or b? Discuss your choices.

1. a. a place for animals to live
    b. a place for people to put their garbage
2. a. a clean ocean and beach
    b. an oil refinery
3. a. a natural forest
    b. a chemical factory
4. a. a marshland
    b. an airport

B.   You are on a special United Nations Commission on Pollution. Talk about the following questions and discuss your answers together.

1.   What are the pollution problems in your country?
2.   What is your government doing about it?
3.   Compare the pollution problems in your country with the United States or another country.
4.   How have pollution problems changed over the last 100 years?
5.   What can we do to clean up and prevent pollution?
6.   What will happen to the earth if we do not stop polluting the environment?

C.   Circle A (*agree*) or D (*disagree*) for the following statements. Compare and discuss your answers with a partner.

OPINION SURVEY

A D   1. Civilization creates pollution.

A D   2. We need chemicals to live better.

A D   3. We can live without cars.

A D   4. There are too many people for the world.

A D   5. The oceans will never get polluted.

A D   6. Noise pollution does not harm anyone.

A D   7. Wild animals have a right to live.

A D   8. People produce too much garbage.

A D   9. If we want cleaner air, we have to give up some conveniences.

A D 10. Chemical plants are as safe as other factories.

Let's Write about It

A.   Write about the changes between pictures a and b at the beginning of this unit.
EXAMPLE: *There was a field with pretty flowers, but now there is a garbage dump there.*

1. _____

2. _____

3. _____

B.   The following letter appeared in *The Daily Post*. Write a response letter to the editor.

> 05/12/1999
>
> Dear Editor:
>   Everyone is talking about pollution. I don't understand why. I know that the air is sometimes dirty, but that's the price we pay for living well. Without cars, planes, and chemicals, where would we be? They make our lives more comfortable. Many people in the world today are worse off than we are. A little pollution is okay with me as long as we stay on top.
>   Sincerely,
>   Unworried about Pollution

_____ ,

_____

_____

_____

_____

_____

_____

_____

Let's Read about It

Poison Gas Leak

On December 2, 1984, one of the worst industrial accidents in history happened in Bhopal, India. A poisonous gas, methyl isocyanate, escaped from a pesticide factory operated by Union Carbide, an American company. While the people living nearby slept, the gas spread quietly over the surrounding countryside. More than 2,000 people died almost immediately as a result of breathing the gas. Another 200,000 suffered serious injuries. In addition, thousands of animals died. The area surrounding the chemical plant became a ghost town. Authorities think that an unhappy worker deliberately caused the leak by opening a valve.

Doctors say that those people who did not die from the chemical will suffer for the rest of their lives. Many have already become blind. Others will probably lose their sight. Many will develop lung problems.

AP/Wide World Photos

Union Carbide realizes the seriousness of this terrible accident. They have made several offers to pay for the damage and to compensate the victims. But how much money is a human life worth?

EXERCISES

A. Match the following expressions.

_____	1. intentionally	a.	ghost town
_____	2. become blind	b.	compensate
_____	3. chemical to kill insects	c.	deliberately
_____	4. pay for damage	d.	lose eyesight
_____	5. a town where people no longer live	e.	accident
_____	6. event causing harm or death	f.	pesticide
_____	7. inhale	g.	happened
_____	8. employee	h.	terrible
_____	9. bad	i.	breathe
_____	10. took place	j.	worker

B. Answer the following questions.

1. What is methyl isocyanate?
2. Where is Bhopal?
3. When did this accident happen?
4. How many people died?
5. How many people were injured?
6. How did the gas escape?
7. Who owns the chemical factory?
8. What kind of medical problems will many people have?
9. What happened to the area surrounding the chemical plant?
10. How did the company try to help the victims?

UNIT 15

EMERGENCY!

Let's Look at It

What is an emergency?
Are the emergencies on this page life threatening?
Do you know what to do in each emergency?

1. Choking

2. Drowning

3. Broken Leg

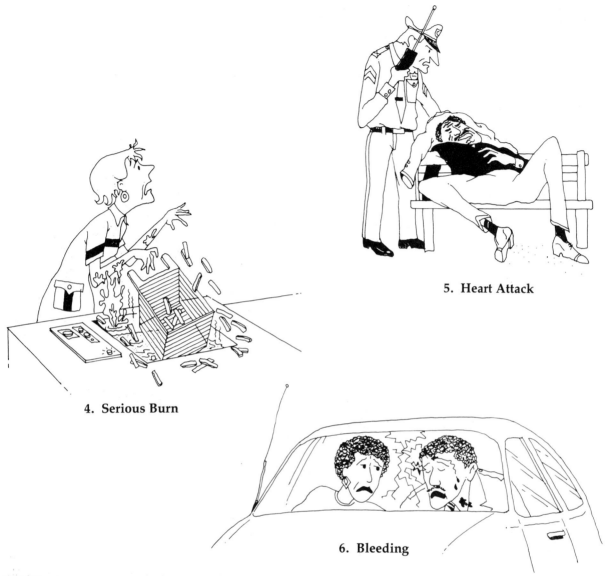

5. **Heart Attack**

4. **Serious Burn**

6. **Bleeding**

VOCABULARY

A.   Match the following words with their meanings.

_____	1. burn	a.	serious, possibly causing death
_____	2. bleed	b.	die by taking water into the lungs
_____	3. choke	c.	special help in a medical emergency
_____	4. drown	d.	block the throat opening
_____	5. heart attack	e.	lose blood
_____	6. broken leg	f.	physical harm
_____	7. life threatening	g.	feel pain
_____	8. injury	h.	sudden, irregular beating of the heart
_____	9. first aid	i.	damage to skin from hot liquid or fire
_____	10. hurt	j.	fractured bone

B.   Fill in the blanks with the following words and expressions.

in pain   broken leg   choking   comfortable   drowning
bleeding   throat   injury   burn   heart attack

1.   The man at the bus stop is having a _____ _____, and the

     police officer is trying to make him _____.

2.   The young man in the skiing accident is _____ _____ because

     he probably has a _____ _____.

3.   The child in the pool is in danger of _____ if the lifeguard doesn't save her.

4.   The woman in the restaurant is _____ because she has some food in her

     _____.

5.   The man in the car accident is _____ from a head _____.

6.   The young woman in the restaurant kitchen is _____ _____

     because of the _____ from hot oil.

Let's Talk about It

A.   *True* (T), *False* (F), or *I don't know.*

_____   1.   All these emergencies are life threatening.

_____   2.   The woman in the car accident is not injured.

_____   3.   Both of the skiiers have broken legs.

_____   4.   A police officer is having a heart attack in emergency 5.

_____   5.   The woman in emergency 4 was burned by fire.

_____   6.   The woman in emergency 1 cannot speak.

_____ 7.   The child in the pool cannot swim well.

_____ 8.   Only two of these emergencies involve children.

_____ 9.   Two of these emergencies are happening in a restaurant.

_____ 10. The heart attack victim is with his wife.

B.   Where is each emergency? Match the following.

_____	1. the young woman	a. in or at the swimming pool
_____	2. the skiers	b. in a restaurant
_____	3. the heart attack victim	c. in the woods
_____	4. the drowning child	d. at a bus stop
_____	5. the choking woman	e. in a car
_____	6. the bleeding person	f. in a house
_____	7. the police officer	
_____	8. the lifeguard	
_____	9. the man with a head injury	

C.   What *might happen* in each emergency?

Example: *The woman in the restaurant might choke to death if someone doesn't help her.*

Some Possibilities	Needed Action
woman . . . choke to death	someone to help her
child . . . drown	the lifeguard to save her
skier . . . lose his leg	his friend to take him to a doctor
old man . . . die	the police officer to call an ambulance
driver . . . bleed to death	someone to stop the bleeding
the woman . . . have scars	someone to put cold water on the burn

D.   What *should* you do for someone in these preceding emergency situations?

EXAMPLE: *You should call an ambulance for anyone who is having a heart attack.*

Let's Read about It

Read the following ways of helping a person (a victim) in an emergency. This kind of help is called first aid. Tell which emergency each paragraph refers to.

1. Apply something cold immediately. This reduces the amount of skin damage and eases the pain. Do not burst any blisters that may form. See a physician if the burn is serious. Take aspirin for pain.

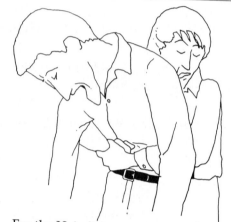

2. For the Heimlich maneuver, stand behind the victim and wrap your arms around his or her waist. Make a fist with one hand and place it, thumb inside, just below the victim's rib cage. Hold your fist with the other hand, and press into the victim's upper stomach with a quick upward movement. Repeat the movement until the object comes out.

3. Put an ice bag on the painful area. If you have to move the victim, make a splint—a support from a rolled-up newspaper, a broom stick, or a board—to keep the broken bone from moving. Tie the splint around the broken bone so that it reaches beyond the joint above and below the break. Do not try to straighten the broken bone. Get the victim to a doctor.

4. With the victim's face down, clear the water from the throat, nose, and mouth. Then, turn the victim on his or her back and, start mouth-to-mouth breathing: Blow one hard breath each five seconds into an adult victim's mouth and one small breath every three seconds for children. Continue this until the victim begins to breathe.

5. The victim may have pain in the chest, neck, or arms, or may have trouble breathing. Call an ambulance and, if you can, the victim's doctor. Make the victim comfortable, but do not make him or her lie down if there is shortness of breath. Do not attempt to lift the victim or make him or her drink anything. Try to calm the victim.

6. Have the victim lie down. To stop the bleeding, firmly press a cloth over the cut. Do not lift the cloth. If the cloth gets bloody, put a fresh cloth over it and continue pressure. If the bleeding is on an arm or leg, apply a tourniquet, a cloth tied on the upper arm or leg, if it does not stop.

EXERCISES

A. In the reading, find another way to say these expressions.

1. do not break any blisters
2. by moving upward quickly
3. a cloth tied tightly to slow blood circulation
4. get the water out of the throat and nose
5. if the victim has trouble breathing
6. in order to make the bleeding stop

B. Match the first aid with the emergency.

_____ 1. broken bone	a. clear the air passage
_____ 2. burn	b. apply something cold
_____ 3. choking	c. start mouth-to-mouth breathing
_____ 4. drowning	d. make a splint
_____ 5. bleeding	e. do not make the victim lie down if breathing is difficult
_____ 6. heart attack	f. stand behind the victim and make a fist
	g. do not straighten the bone
	h. do not give anything to drink
	i. push upward quickly in the upper stomach
	j. tie a tourniquet above the injury

C. Answer these questions.

1. Why should you apply something cold to a burn?
2. What are the symptoms of a heart attack?
3. How do you give mouth-to-mouth breathing to an adult? to a child?
4. What is the Heimlich maneuver? How do you do it?
5. How do you stop bleeding?
6. How long do you apply the Heimlich maneuver? mouth-to-mouth breathing?

Let's Talk about It Again

Answer these questions. In groups, discuss your answers.

1. Which emergency seems the most serious? the least serious?
2. Which form of first aid seems the easiest? the most difficult?
3. Which emergencies require the victim to lie down for first aid?
4. Which emergencies require a tourniquet?
5. Which emergencies happen mostly to children? to adults?
6. Are you familiar with an emergency like one of these? If you are, tell what happened.

Let's Write about It

A. Write a sentence about what might happen to each person if he or she doesn't get help.

1. _____

2. _____

3. _____

4. _____

5. _____

6. _____

B. Write a sentence about what you should do to help each person with an emergency.

1. _____

2. _____

3. _____

4. _____

5. _____

6. _____

C. Imagine you helped one of these people. Write about what you did. Or if you have ever had an emergency, write about it.

How I Helped Someone in an Emergency

_____

_____

_____

_____

UNIT 16

BOMB ON BOARD!

Let's Look at It

How do you feel about flying?
What are some of the dangers?
What is skyjacking?

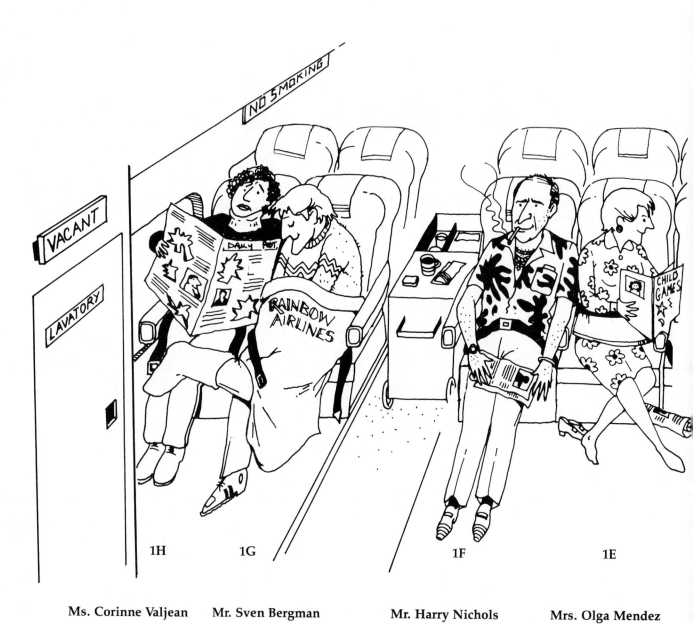

1H   1G   1F   1E

Ms. Corinne Valjean   Mr. Sven Bergman   Mr. Harry Nichols   Mrs. Olga Mendez

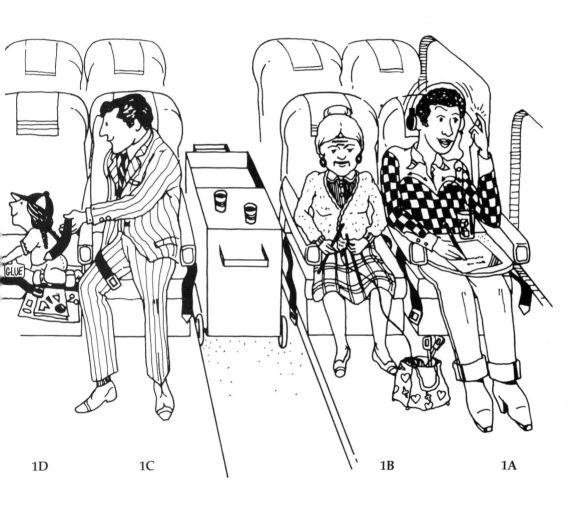

1D   1C   1B   1A

Millie Mendez   Mr. Carlos Mendez   Mrs. Roberta Whitlock   Mr. Ali Mansour

VOCABULARY

A.   Circle the actions that you see in the picture.

a) sleeping   b) smoking   c) walking   d) reading   e) writing   f) drinking

g) knitting   h) skiing   i) sitting   j) listening to music   k) dancing

l) playing with paper and glue   m) fastening a seat belt

B.   Match the following. (Some numbers have more than one answer and some letters are used more than once.)

_____ 1.	Mr. Mansour	a.	sitting next to a window
_____ 2.	Mrs. Whitlock	b.	sitting on the aisle
_____ 3.	Mr. Mendez	c.	sitting between two adults
_____ 4.	Mrs. Mendez	d.	has the seat belt fastened
_____ 5.	Millie Mendez	e.	wearing jeans
_____ 6.	Mr. Nichols	f.	has the seat belt unfastened
_____ 7.	Mr. Bergman	g.	is the oldest
_____ 8.	Ms. Valjean	h.	is the youngest
		i.	has scissors
		j.	has a newspaper with holes in it
		k.	has a broken leg

C.   Now, without looking back, try to remember what each person is doing. Discuss your answers.

Mr. Mansour   Mrs. Whitlock   Mr. Mendez   Mrs. Mendez

Millie Mendez   Mr. Nichols   Mr. Bergman   Ms. Valjean

Let's Talk about It

A.   Look carefully at the scene on pages 132 and 133. Answer these questions.

1.   Who is probably traveling together?
2.   Who probably know each other?
3.   Who can't move about easily?
4.   Who is doing something that is not allowed?
5.   Who seems the most relaxed? The most nervous?
6.   What is each person doing?

B. Use *can* or *can't* in these sentences and give the reasons.

1. Ms. Valjean _____ hear Mr. Mansour's music because _____ .

2. Mr. Bergman _____ easily get up and walk about because _____ .

3. Mrs. Whitlock _____ knit very fast because _____ .

4. Mr. Mansour _____ move easily from his seat because _____ .

5. Mr. Bergman _____ walk easily because _____ .

6. Ms. Valjean _____ read all the news in the newspaper because

    _____ .

7. Millie Mendez _____ see out the window because _____ .

8. Mr. Mendez _____ fasten his seat belt right now because _____ .

C.   Do you remember? Without looking back, describe these people.

1. The person sitting by the left window.
2. The person sitting by the right window.
3. The person sitting in seat 1B.
4. The person sitting between Millie Mendez and Mr. Nichols.
5. The young couple.
6. The family.

Let's Read about It

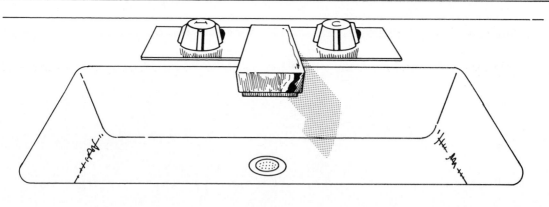

A. A flight attendant, Ruby Bird, finds this note in a front restroom of the plane. She goes immediately to Captain Swift, the pilot. Read the conversation on the next page and put the statements in order. Use numbers.

* Miss Bird   # Captain Swift

_____ # Someone cut out different newspaper letters and glued them on a sheet of company
stationery. The glue's not dry yet.

_____ # What does it say, Miss Bird?

_____ * Sure. Here it is.

_____ # A bomb? Let me take a look at that note.

_____ * You know, Captain, the stationery is free to
anyone who asks. And most of the passengers have newspapers.

___1___ * Captain Swift, look at this note. It was on the mirror in the front restroom.

_____ # But where did the glue come from?

_____ # That's all true, but you can't put together a note like this on an airplane without
someone seeing you.

_____ * Oh, a little girl is playing with some now.

_____ * What can we do, Captain? Do you want me to tell the passengers?

_____ * It says there's a bomb on the plane.

_____ # I suppose so.

_____ # No. I'll radio for instructions. Go back and act calmly.

_____ * Oh, yes, it's possible. In the restroom. Some of the passengers were in there a long
time.

B.   Underline the correct answer(s).

1.   (Miss Bird, Captain Swift, another passenger) finds the note.
2.   Someone leaves the note in the (restroom, aisle, plane, seat).
3.   In order to prepare the note, someone uses (scissors, a pen, glue, stationery, a newspaper).
4.   Captain Swift plans to (ask for instructions, contact the airport, go back and act calmly, pay the money).
5.   The glue comes from (the woman who is knitting, the man who is listening to music, the little girl who is playing, the young man who is sleeping).

Let's Talk about It Again

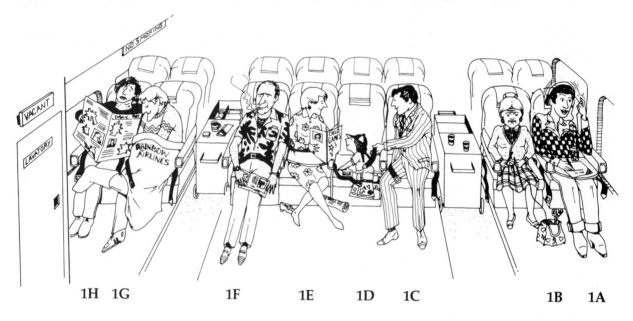

1H   1G   1F   1E   1D   1C   1B   1A

A.   Look at the picture and read the dialogue on page 137 again. Who has the glue? The newspaper? The scissors? The stationery?

B.   Ruby Bird knows that one of the eight people in the first row placed the note in the restroom. They were the only ones free to go to the front restroom because the aisles behind that row were blocked. Flight attendants were serving food in both aisles. Answer these questions. Compare your answers with other students.

1.   Who can get up and move around easily?
2.   Why can't the others move easily?
3.   Which things did the passenger use to prepare the note?
4.   Where did that person get these things?
5.   Where did that person prepare the note?
6.   Why do you think this person did this?
7.   Where do you think the bomb is?
8.   Who do you think left the note in the restroom?

Let's Write about It

A.   Write five sentences about what is happening in the airplane.

1. _____

2. _____

3. _____

4. _____

5. _____

B.   Here are some notes that Ruby Bird wrote. Finish the note and include your solution to the mystery.

Rainbow Airlines

I'm waiting for the Captain
to make his announcement,
and I'm trying to keep calm.
Right now everyone else
is quiet. There is no excitement
yet. Mrs. Mendez is still...

_____

_____

_____

_____

C. Now write a similar paragraph about what's happening around you right now.

UNIT 17

WHITE LIES

Let's Look at It

What are white lies?
Do you ever tell white lies?
What do you think of people who tell white lies?

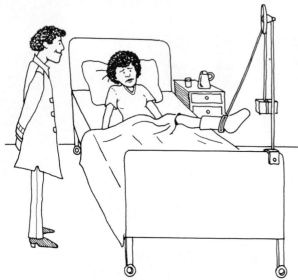

1. **Brendan**: You look good in white, May.
    (Poor gal. It's too bad she's in
    such bad shape.)
    May: You say the nicest things.

2. **Mollie**: Your son is such a creative child.
    (How can she put up with that
    brat!)
    Mildred: Yes, he *does* have artistic
    talent.

4. **Michael**: Well, how do you like my
    Mohawk haircut?
    Peter: Um. It looks great.
    (Ugh! Is he crazy?)

3. **Robin**: What do you think of Harold, my
    pet snake?
    Cathy: He's quite, uh, attractive.
    (How can he stand that cold
    creature on his neck?)

5. **Flo**: You seem very busy today.
   (How can he find anything in
   that mess?)
   Ed: I'm up to my neck in work.

6. **Daisy**: I've just had my portrait painted.
   Carmen: It's just lovely.
   (If she hadn't told me, I
   wouldn't have recognized
   her!)

7. **Diego**: Would you like to go to the
   movies with me tonight?
   Gloria: I'd love to, but I've made other
   plans.
   (I wish he'd stop asking me to go
   out with him!)

VOCABULARY

A. Match the following words with the words or expressions that are nearly the same in meaning.

_____	1. neat	a.	pretty or handsome
_____	2. have artistic talent	b.	a child who is not well behaved
_____	3. portrait	c.	an animal
_____	4. in bad shape	d.	a type of haircut
_____	5. creative	e.	with everything in order
_____	6. brat	f.	painting or picture of someone
_____	7. attractive	g.	not in good health
_____	8. creature	h.	making new things or ideas
_____	9. Mohawk	i.	be good in drawing
_____	10. lovely	j.	nice or pleasant

B. Write the number of the situation which refers to the following.

_____ 1. He is very busy.   _____ 5. He got an unusual haircut.

_____ 2. She has a broken leg.   _____ 6. She has an active son.

_____ 3. He has a pet snake.   _____ 7. He likes Gloria.

_____ 4. She has a new portrait.

Let's Talk about It

A. Look at each of the pictures and report what the people said.

EXAMPLE: *Brendan said that May looked good in white.*

B. Look at each picture and report what the people really thought. People's thoughts appear in parentheses.

EXAMPLE: *Brendan thought that May was in bad shape.*

C. Now combine what each person said with what they really thought.

EXAMPLE: *Although Brendan said that May looked good in white, he really thought she was in bad shape.*

D. In your opinion, why didn't these people say what they thought? Discuss the reasons in groups.

E. *Role play*: With another student practice your own conversations in each of the situations below. Use this sequence in your conversation:

First person: *Ask for an opinion* or *a favor*.
Second person: *Say something nice.* (On a piece of paper write down what you really think.)

THE SITUATIONS:

1. A friend who has a new boyfriend or girlfriend.

2. A friend who bought an old, rusty car.

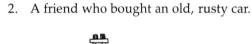

3. A friend who wants to borrow some money.

4. Friends who think their house is beautiful.

5. A friend who has an unusual pet.

6. A friend who has new glasses.

F. Circle A (*agree*) or D (*disagree*) for the following statements. Discuss your answers with a partner.

OPINION SURVEY

A D 1. Most people always say what they think.

A D 2. The truth hurts.

A D 3. It's best always to be honest when you speak.

A D 4. Most people want to hear the truth.

A D 5. Most people want to hear pleasant things, not necessarily the truth.

A D 6. You can always find something nice to say to someone.

A D 7. White lies don't really hurt anyone.

A D 8. A real friend will always tell you the truth.

A D 9. Everyone tells white lies now and then.

A D 10. People who tell white lies are dishonest.

G. Discuss the following:

1. An occasion when you or someone you know told a white lie.
2. The attitudes of the people in your country toward white lies.
3. Why do some people tell white lies?
4. Why do some people tell real lies?

Let's Write about It

A. Report in writing what four people said in the first situations.

1. _____

2. _____

3. _____

4. _____

B.   Report in writing what four people thought in the first situations.

1.   _____

2.   _____

3.   _____

4.   _____

C.   Report in writing what four people said and thought in the first situations.

1.   _____

2.   _____

3.   _____

4.   _____

D.   You have just received the following wedding invitation. You *do not* want to attend. Write a response that will not hurt the feelings of Mrs. and Mrs. Patton.

Mr. and Mrs. David Patton request

the honor of your presence at the marriage

of their daughter Patricia Lucille

to Mr. William B. Percey

on Saturday, April 25, at four in the afternoon.

R.S.V.P.

_____

_____

_____

Let's Read about It

Lies Can Hurt

White lies—when we don't tell the truth because we don't want to hurt someone's feelings—don't usually hurt people. However, real lies do. A dangerous situation sometimes results when people tell lies, particularly about their professional education.

One famous case involved a man who said he studied meteorology at a large university. He had a job forecasting the weather on the radio, where he worked for seven years. Someone finally discovered his lie by checking the records at the university. This man never studied there. He was just a high school graduate. His weather forecasts were only guesses.

There are also many other cases where people have lied about their professional background. Phony "lawyers" have opened offices and given legal advice to innocent clients and represented them in court. The clients, of course, did not know that they were dealing with phonies. The clients then had legal problems for years.

The most dangerous cases, however, involve people who claim they are medical doctors. In recent years there have been several cases of people who said they were graduates of medical schools. They worked as doctors in hospitals. They prescribed medicine and performed operations on patients. Many innocent people were hurt because these "doctors" knew very little about medicine.

It is a good idea to check with medical or legal organizations if you have questions or complaints about your doctor or lawyer. An honest person has nothing to fear from the truth.

EXERCISES

A.   Find and write the words in the passage that have the following meanings:

1.   not real
2.   study of weather
3.   wrote out instructions (for medicine)
4.   to predict
5.   to contact
6.   customer (to a lawyer)
7.   not guilty or without experience
8.   customer (to a doctor)

B.   Answer the following questions:

1.   What's the difference between white lies and real lies?
2.   How was the phony meteorologist discovered?
3.   Why did the clients of the phony lawyers have legal problems later?
4.   Why are phony doctors the most dangerous?
5.   What can you do about phony doctors or lawyers?

UNIT 18

UNDER THE INFLUENCE

Let's Look at It

Have you ever seen an auto accident?
Do you know anyone who drinks and drives?
Do you know anyone who was injured by a drunk driver?

Maureen: Hello, John. I need your help.
John: Maureen, what's wrong?
Maureen: I was in an accident, and I'm at the police station. I think I'm in serious trouble.
John: What happened?
Maureen: I was driving home from a party. It was late and dark and I couldn't see clearly. A boy on a
      bike rode out in front of me. I couldn't stop.
John: Was the boy injured?
Maureen: Yes. The police arrested me. They think I had too much to drink. They gave me some kind of
      test. They made me blow into a machine.
John: A breathalizer test?
Maureen: Yes, that's it. I need a lawyer. Please come right away.
John: Don't say anything else, Maureen. I'll be right there.

VOCABULARY

A.   Match the following words and expressions.

_____	1. arrest	a.	wasn't able
_____	2. breathalizer	b.	consumed too much alcohol
_____	3. injured	c.	put in jail
_____	4. accident	d.	machine to measure alcohol
_____	5. couldn't	e.	hurt
_____	6. else	f.	an unplanned injury or damage
_____	7. right away	g.	immediately
_____	8. too much to drink	h.	more

B.   What happened first? Place the following events in the correct sequence. Use numbers.

_____ The police arrested Maureen.

_____ Maureen called John.

_____ Maureen took a breathalizer test.

_____ A boy was injured.

_____ Maureen was driving home from a party.

__1__ Maureen was at a party.

_____ John said he'd come to the police station.

_____ Maureen hit the boy on the bicycle.

_____ The ambulance came and took the boy to a hospital.

Let's Talk about It

A.   Answer these questions individually. Then compare and discuss your answers.

1.   Do you feel sorry for Maureen? Why?
2.   Do you feel sorry for the boy? Why?
3.   Where was Maureen before the accident?
4.   Why do you think the boy was out so late?
5.   According to Maureen, what caused the accident?
6.   According to the police, what caused the accident?
7.   Why did John tell Maureen *not* to say anything else?
8.   Do you think that Maureen is guilty or innocent?

B.   Role Play: Trial by jury

A jury must decide whether or not Maureen is guilty of driving under the influence of alcohol. Select one person in the class to be the *defendant*, one person to be the *defense attorney*, and one person to be the *prosecutor*. The rest of the class will be the *jury*.

Defendant
Name: Maureen Jenkins
Age: 28
Occupation: Teacher
Charge: Driving under the influence of alcohol
Plea: Not guilty.

Prosecutor
Name: Judith Upright
Age: 33

Prosecution Argument:
The prosecuting attorney will make these points during the trial. Decide in pairs if the statement is *valid* (it is fair to make this point) or *invalid* (it isn't fair to make this point). Then discuss your answers in groups. Each group must come to the same decision.

	Valid	Invalid
1. Maureen was drinking alcohol at the party.	_____	_____
2. She failed a breathalizer test.	_____	_____

3. Alcohol slows reaction time. _____ _____

4. She is short and thin, so she needs very little alcohol to get

drunk. _____ _____

5. If she had not been drinking, she could have stopped in time. _____ _____

6. She is not an experienced driver. _____ _____

7. She's doesn't know how to handle alcohol. _____ _____

8. She's a woman driver. _____ _____

Other arguments _____

_____

Defense Attorney
Name: John Sobre
Age: 42

Defense Argument:
The defense attorney will make these points during the trial. Decide in pairs if the statement is *valid* or *invalid*. Then discuss your decisions in groups. Each group must have the same decision.

	Valid	Invalid
1. It was dark and late.	_____	_____
2. The boy was wearing dark clothing.	_____	_____
3. The boy was on the wrong side of the road.	_____	_____
4. It was too late for the boy to be out.	_____	_____
5. Maureen said she wasn't drunk.	_____	_____
6. The breathalizer test is not always accurate.	_____	_____

7. Maureen was tired—not drunk.   _____ _____

8. Maureen only drank two glasses of wine.   _____ _____

Other arguments _____

_____

D. Discuss the prosecution and defense arguments and decide:

1. Which side you agree with.
2. Who is responsible for causing the accident.
3. If Maureen is guilty of drunk driving.
    Note: To be guilty, the verdict must be unanimous—that is, everyone must agree!
4. What should the punishment be if she is guilty? She *should*
    a. lose her driver's license.
    b. go to prison.   If so, for how long?
    c. pay a lot of money as a fine. If so, how much?
    d. pay the boy's medical expenses.
    e. help other people with drinking problems.

E. Circle A (*agree*) or D (*disagree*) for the following statements. Discuss your answers with a partner.

OPINION SURVEY

A D 1.   Drunk drivers don't know what they are doing.

A D 2.   Drunk drivers should attend special classes.

A D 3.   Punishing drunk drivers will not stop accidents.

A D 4.   The licenses of drunk drivers should be taken away.

A D 5.   Drunk drivers are sick; they are not criminals.

A D 6.   Drunk drivers should receive a fair trial before being punished.

A D 7.   Only prison sentences will discourage drunk driving.

A D 8.   Some people can drink more than others and not get drunk.

A D 9.   Drunk drivers hurt themselves more than they hurt others.

A D 10. The government should not give driver's licenses to people who drink.

Let's Write about It

A.   Write three facts against Maureen that you remember from the accident.

EXAMPLE: *She failed the breathalizer test.*

1. _____

2. _____

3. _____

B.   Write three facts in Maureen's favor that you remember.

EXAMPLE: *It was dark.*

1. _____

2. _____

3. _____

C.   Finish the following police report. Give the details of the accident: what happened, the time, who was involved, who was injured, and why Maureen was taken to the police station.

POLICE REPORT   DATE: _____

                                 TIME: _____

_____

_____

_____

_____

_____

_____

Let's Read about It

Too Drunk to Drive?

Drunk driving is the leading cause of death for young people between the ages of 18 and 21 in the United States. It does not take much to become too drunk to drive. The following chart illustrates the relationship between the number of drinks, body weight, and blood alcohol level.

W. Marc Bernsau/The Image Works

WEIGHT (in pounds)

		120	140	160	180	200	220
D	1	.03	.03	.02	.02	.02	.02
R	2	.06	.05	.05	.04	.04	.03
I	3	.09	.08	.07	.06	.06	.05
N	4	.12	.11	.09	.08	.08	.07
K	5	.16	.13	.12	.11	.09	.09
S	6	.19	.16	.14	.13	.11	.10

BLOOD ALCOHOL LEVELS

(Source: American Medical Association)

Blood alcohol level is measured by a device called the breathalizer. It is unsafe to drive a car if your blood alcohol level is .10 or higher. If you are stopped by the police and your blood alcohol level is above .10, you will be arrested. At this level your probability of causing an accident is 8 percent. As the blood alcohol level increases, your probability of causing an accident increases dramatically; for example, with a blood alcohol level of .15, the probability of causing an accident rises to 25 percent, and at .20, the probability shoots to over 50 percent.

If you drink, do not drive. It is illegal and dangerous to yourself and to others. You could wind up in jail, or worse yet, you could kill yourself or an innocent person. If you have to get home, call a relative or friend. The life you save may be your own.

EXERCISES

A.   Answer *true* or *false* or *I don't know*.

_____   1.   If you have one drink, it is unsafe to drive.

_____   2.   If the police stop you for drunk driving, they will take you home.

_____   3.   You have a 50 percent chance of causing an accident if your blood alcohol level is .20.

_____   4.   Never let anyone know when you are too drunk to drive.

_____   5.   Most drunk drivers never get caught.

_____   6.   The breathalizer is not accurate.

_____   7.   Most deaths from drunk driving are among young people.

_____   8.   Some people can drink and not be too drunk to drive.

B.   Answer the following questions:

1.   What could happen if you drink and drive?
2.   What is the leading cause of death among young people?
3.   How many drinks can people who weigh 160 pounds have before their blood alcohol level is unsafe?
4.   At what blood alcohol level are *you* considered drunk?
5.   What is the relationship between having a car accident and the amount of alcohol in your blood?
6.   What should you do if you drink too much?

UNIT 19

WHO KILLED FARMER BROWN?

Let's Look at It

Is murder the most serious of crimes?
Why do people commit murder?
What should society do to punish a murderer?

Farmer Murdered

Barrington, Sept. 10. Anatoly S. Brown, 70, a retired farmer, was found dead outside his house last night. The house was ransacked. A heavy stone was next to his body. The police believe that the murderer used this stone to kill Mr. Brown sometime around 9:30 P.M. They are questioning a number of suspects.

Mr. Brown came to this country from the U.S.S.R. over twenty years ago. Even though he never learned to read and write English, he changed his name to Anatoly S. Brown from the Russian ANATOLY SERGEEVICH BURY.

АНАТОЛИЙ СЕРГЕЕВИЧ БУРЫЙ

Mr. Brown lived alone. His neighbors did not know much about him. They thought he was poor, so they often brought him food.

After he died, the police learned that he had $270,000 in the bank, but his bank book was missing. Due to booming development, his land is worth more than $1,000,000. Over the years several people offered to buy his land, but he refused to sell. The police investigation is continuing.

VOCABULARY

A. Match the following words and phrases with words that have the same meaning in the article.

_____	1. kill	a.	ransacked
_____	2. not working anymore	b.	is continuing
_____	3. rock	c.	worth
_____	4. not there	d.	refused
_____	5. fast growing	e.	murder
_____	6. new houses under construction	f.	stone
_____	7. valued at	g.	booming
_____	8. didn't want to	h.	missing
_____	9. not finished	i.	retired
_____	10. everything thrown about	j.	development

B. Fill in the missing words.

(1) The police think that Mr. Brown was _____. (2) They think the murder weapon was a large _____. (3) Most of Mr. Brown's neighbors thought he was _____ although he had a lot of _____ in the bank, but his bank book was _____. (4) Mr. Brown's farm was _____ a lot of money—over one million dollars. (5) Actually, Mr. Brown was not so _____. (6) The police are still _____ the mysterious murder case.

Let's Talk about It

A. *True* or *false* or *I don't know?*

_____ 1. Mr. Brown was a nice man.

_____ 2. Mr. Brown was killed with a gun.

_____ 3. Mr. Brown lived with his son.

_____ 4. The neighbors thought Mr. Brown had no food.

_____ 5. Mr. Brown came to this country when he was very young.

_____ 6. The police finished their investigation.

_____ 7. Mr. Brown was an immigrant from Russia.

_____ 8. Mr. Brown knew Russian.

B.   Answer these questions.

1. Where did the police find Mr. Brown?
2. What did they find beside the body?
3. What is surprising about Mr. Brown's financial status?
4. How much money did he have in the bank?
5. Why did the neighbors bring him food?
6. Who lived with Mr. Brown?
7. How did Mr. Brown die?
8. What do you see in the picture *not* mentioned in the newspaper article?

The Suspects

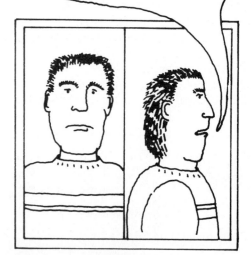

Name: Pasha Bury Coontz
Age: 65
Marital status: Married, husband unemployed
Occupation: Secretary to Plato Carpov
Relationship to Mr. Brown: Sister
Motive: Will get Mr. Brown's farm and money. She has agreed to sell the farm to Mr. Carpov in the event of Mr. Brown's death.

Name: Rudolph Sigmon
Age: Late twenties
Marital Status: Single
Occupation: Farm hand
Relationship to Mr. Brown: Worked on Mr. Brown's farm.
Motive: Thought Mr. Brown had money hidden in the house.

Name: Plato Carpov
Age: 46
Marital Status: Married, two children
Occupation: Owner of a nearby housing
                      development
Relationship to Mr. Brown: Neighbor
Motive: Wanted Mr. Brown's land to expand his
            housing development, but Mr. Brown
            refused to sell it to him.

Name: Raisa Stolichnaya
Age: Early twenties
Marital Status: Divorced, no children
Occupation: Waitress
Relationship to Mr. Brown: Girlfriend
Motive: She knew how much money he had.
            Rudolph introduced Raisa to Mr.
            Brown.

C.   Match the following. More than one answer is possible in some cases.

_____ 1. worked for Farmer Brown	a. Pasha Bury Coontz
_____ 2. was married	b. Rudolph Sigmon
_____ 3. is related to Farmer Brown	c. Plato Carpov
_____ 4. wanted to buy Farmer Brown's land	d. Raisa Stolichnaya
_____ 5. was working during the murder	
_____ 6. knew Farmer Brown had money	
_____ 7. thought Farmer Brown had money	
_____ 8. knew how Farmer Brown was murdered	

D.   Discuss in small groups these questions about the following suspects.

the sister (Pasha Bury Coontz)   the farm hand (Rudolph Sigmon)

the neighbor (Plato Carpov)   the girlfriend (Raisa Stolichnaya)

1.   Which of the suspects had a *motive*, something to gain from killing Farmer Brown?
2.   Which of the suspects had an *alibi*, a reason why he or she could *not* have killed Farmer Brown?
3.   Who was strong enough to lift the large stone to kill Farmer Brown?
4.   Whom do the letters "P.C." refer to? In Russian, what sounds do these letters have?
5.   Which person do you think killed Farmer Brown? Explain why you think so.

E.   In many countries, murderers receive the death penalty. Circle A (*agree*) or D (*disagree*) with the following statements about murder and the death penalty. Discuss your answers.

OPINION SURVEY

A   D   1.   The death penalty is cruel and inhuman.

A   D   2.   The death penalty does not stop people from murdering.

A   D   3.   People still killed even when the death penalty was used a lot.

A   D   4.   The state practices murder when it executes murderers.

A   D   5.   There are more effective ways than the death penalty to punish murderers.

A   D   6.   Life in prison is a more terrible penalty than death.

A   D   7.   Killing another person in a war is not the same as murder.

A   D   8.   Killing to protect oneself is sometimes necessary.

F.   Should the death penalty be used in all cases where one person kills another person? Discuss with your group what kind of punishment should be given to the "killers" in the following situations.

1.   A driver who loses control of his car and kills a child.
2.   A bank robber who kills a bank employee.
3.   A girl playing with a gun who kills her brother.
4.   A wife or husband who poisons the other because of jealousy.
5.   A store owner who kills a robber.

6. A policeman who kills a prisoner escaping from a prison.
7. A homeowner who kills a burglar.
8. A doctor who kills a suffering patient.

Let's Write about It

A. Who murdered Farmer Brown? Why? Write one sentence.

1. _____ because _____

B. Who couldn't have murdered Farmer Brown? Why? Write three sentences.

1. _____ because _____

2. _____ because _____

3. _____ because _____

C. Who could have murdered Farmer Brown but didn't?

_____ because _____

C. Write a paragraph by answering the following questions in complete sentences.

Who Killed Farmer Brown?

1. Was it late at night?
2. Was Mr. Brown at home alone?
3. Did he hear a noise outside?
4. Did he walk outside to take a look?
5. Did someone hit him in the head with a large stone?
6. As he was dying, did he write something in the dirt?
7. Are there a number of suspects?
8. Do you know the name of the killer?

_____

_____

_____

_____

_____

Let's Read about It

A Cruel and Unusual Punishment

The death penalty is an inhuman form of punishment. Civilized people should not punish murderers this way. It doesn't even work. It does not stop people from committing murder. The death penalty has existed for centuries, but people still kill one another.

When a brutal criminal is put to death, some people are happy because they think that justice was done. What they don't realize is that by executing criminals, the state practices the kind of behavior it wants to punish. The state becomes a murderer, too. Two "wrongs" don't make a "right." Justice is not always perfect. Cases exist where the state executed an innocent person. Once a life is taken, you cannot bring it back.

Today the death penalty is not necessary because there are better ways to punish killers. Much worse than death is knowing that you are going to spend the rest of your life in prison with no hope of getting out. Life in prison is a more terrible punishment because the murderers must live with the memory and guilt of their crime.

To the Editor:

Crime is out of control. Every day we read in your newspaper stories of horrible murders. It is quite clear that the police cannot be everywhere to protect everyone. The only way to protect honest citizens is to remove murderers permanently from society—like cancer from the body.

In your editorial you say that life in prison is the solution. We know, however, that convicted murderers almost never spend their entire lives in prison. After a few years, they are released and often kill again. Even the murderers of policemen have been freed.

Execution is the only way to stop them—dead!

Harry Iceman

EXERCISES

A. Match the following words and expressions.

_____	1. cruel	a.	kill
_____	2. unusual	b.	not guilty
_____	3. death penalty	c.	brutal
_____	4. civilized	d.	guilty
_____	5. commit murder	e.	polite, not barbarian
_____	6. exist	f.	execution
_____	7. innocent	g.	understand
_____	8. realize	h.	not common
_____	9. convicted	i.	be

B. Choose an answer and then complete these sentences.

1. The death penalty is (necessary/unnecessary) because _____.

2. The death penalty (stops/does not stop) people from committing murder because

    _____.

3. Life in prison (is/is not) a terrible punishment because _____.

4. The death penalty is a (civilized/cruel) form of punishment because _____.

INDEX OF TOPICS

INDEX OF GRAMMATICAL STRUCTURES

INDEX OF LANGUAGE FUNCTIONS

ANSWER KEY

Page	Ex.	
4	A:	1-g, 2-b, 3-f, 4-a, 5-e, 6-c, 7-d, 8-h
	B:	1-animal trainer, 2-trapeze artist, 3-magic, 4-acrobats, 5-clown, 6-Asian, 7-European, 8-North American
8	A:	1-Asia, 2-mice, 3-Texas, 4-helpful, 5-poisonous, 6-ugly
13	A:	1-c, 2-a, 3-c, 4-e, 5-a,b, 6-b, 7-e, 8-d, 9-d
	B:	1-b, 2-c, 3-a, 4-a, 5-c, 6-b, 7-a, 8-c, 9-c
19	A:	1-c, 2-a, 3-c, 4-c, 5-b, 6-b
	B:	1-c, 2-a, 3-b, 4-b, 5-c, 6-a
22	A:	1-c, 2-g, 3-b, 4-h, 5-d, 6-a, 7-f, 8-e
23-24	C:	a-4, b-3, c-5, d-10, e-11, f-2, g-7, h-6, i-8, j-12, k-1, l-9
27	A:	1-14,16, 2-13,14, 3-6,7, 4-23,24,25,26,27, 5-8,9, 6-13
30	A:	1-c, 2-e, 3-a, 4-b, 5-d, 6-g, 7-h, 8-f, 9-j, 10-i
31	B:	1-b, 2-b, 3-a, 4-b, 5-d, 6-b, 7-d, 8-b, 9-b,e, 10-a
36	A:	1-d, 2-c, 3-b, 4-f, 5-g, 6-e, 7-a
40	B:	1-d, 2-h, 3-f, 4-a, 5-b, 6-g, 7-e, 8-c
44	A:	1-expressive, 2-major, 3-abused, 4-silent, 5-recover, 6-violent, 7-benefits
48	A:	1-players, teams, 2-ball, 3-smaller, tennis, 4-field, 5-points, score, 6-boxing, tennis
	B:	1-c, baseball, 2-d, basketball, 3-a, golf, 4-f, boxing, 5-b, football, 6-3, tennis
53	A:	1-fan, 2-fanatic, 3-broke out, 4-violence, 5-instead of, 6-seem crazy, 7-occurred, 8-conflict, 9-collapsed, 10-humble, 11-tragedy
56	A:	1-e, 2-d, 3-a, 4-f, 5-d, 6-d, 7-c, 8-d, 9-c, 10-b
	A:	1-F, 2-T, 3-F, 4-T, 5-T, 6-F
62	A:	1-f, 2-c, 3-a, 4-g, 5-b, 6-d, 7-e
72	A:	1-e, 2-d, 3-i, 4-c, 5-g, 6-b, 7-h, 8-a, 9-f
	B:	1-f, 2-f, 3-f, 4-t, 5-f, 6-f
76	A:	1-d,k; 2-e,g; 3-f,i,q; 4-c,h,l; 5-a,j,m; 6-b,n,o,p
80	A:	a-4,8,9; b-1,5,6; c-2,3,7
	B:	1-d, 2-c, 3-a, 4-e, 5-b
83	A:	1-e, 2-f, 3-b, 4-c, 5-a, 6-d
88	A:	1-b, 2-d, 3-a, 4-g, 5-c, 6-e, 7-f, 8-j, 9-i, 10-h
	B:	1-gamblers, 2-risk, 3-bets, 4-casinos, 5-roulette, 6-blackjack, 7-slot machines, 8-unlucky, 9-sports, 10-won, 11-lucky, 12-gambling, 13-winning
93	A:	1-on top of the world, 2-anonymous, 3-habitual, 4-temptation, 5-shared
	B:	1-f, 2-t, 3-t, 4-f, 5-f, 6-f
98	A:	1-b, 2-d, 3-f, 4-c, 5-a, 6-e
102	A:	1-c, 2-d, 3-b, 4-a, 5-d, 6-b
107	A:	1-license, 2-I won't graduate, 3-bribe, 4-computer, 5-I can arrange it
	B:	1-c, 2-a,e, 3-d,g, 4-f,g, 5-b, 6-a,e
111	A:	1-f, 2-t, 3-f, 4-t, 5-t, 6-t, 7-t, 8-f, 9-t, 10-t
	B:	1-illegal, 2-special favors, 3-punishment, 4-you have to pay a bribe, 5-equal treatment, 6-bribery is dishonest, 7-jet planes, weapons and oil, 8-you "buy" unfair advantage
116	A:	1-2a,2b, 2-1a, 3-3b, 4-3a, 5-1a,1b,4b, 6-1b, 7-2b, 8-4b, 9-4a, 10-1a, 11-1b, 12-2a,2b,4a,4b, 13-2b,4b, 14-4b, 15-4a, 16-4b
	B:	1-c,d, 2-c,d, 3-a,b,d, 4-a,b,d, 5-c, 6-c,d, 7-a,b,c,d, 8-a,b,d
120	A:	1-c, 2-d, 3-f, 4-b, 5-a, 6-e, 7-i, 8-j, 9-h, 10-g
123	A:	1-i, 2-e, 3-d, 4-b, 5-h, 6-j, 7-a, 8-f, 9-c, 10-g
124	B:	1-f,d, 2-a,b, 3-e, 4-c,h, 5-g,i, 6-a,j
127	A:	1-do not burst any blisters, 2-quick upward movement, 3-tourniquet, 4-clear the water, 5-trouble breathing, 6-to stop the bleeding
	B:	1-b,d,g, 2-b, 3-f,i, 4-a,c, 5-j, 6-e
134	A:	a, b, d, e, g, i, j, l, m
	B:	1-a,e,f, 2-i,b,f,g, 3-f,b, 4-d, 5-c,f,h,i, 6-b,f, 7-b,f,k, 8-a,f,j
137	A:	6, 2, 5, 4, 7, 1, 8, 10, 9, 13, 3, 12, 14, 11
144	A:	1-e, 2-i, 3-f, 4-g, 5-h, 6-b, 7-a, 8-c, 9-d, 10-j
	B:	1-5, 2-1, 3-3, 4-6, 5-4, 6-2, 7-7
149	A:	1-phony, 2-meteorology, 3-prescribed medicine, 4-forecast, 5-check with, 6-client, 7-innocent, 8-patient
153	A:	1-c, 2-d, 3-e, 4-f, 5-a, 6-h, 7-g, 8-b
	B:	7, 8, 6, 4, 2, 1, 9, 3, 5
159	A:	1-F, 2-F, 3-T, 4-F, 5-T, 6-F, 7-T, 8-F
163	A:	1-e, 2-i, 3-f, 4-h, 5-g, 6-j, 7-c, 8-d, 9-b, 10-a
	B:	1-murdered, 2-stone, 3-poor, money, missing, 4-worth, 5-poor, 6-investigating
168	A:	1-c, 2-h, 3-f, 4-e, 5-a, 6-i, 7-b, 8-g, 9-d